AF599269

Praise for *My Golf Journey*

Golf is a classy competitive sport that is played with a passion unlike any other game in the world. This astonishing book is about an extraordinary journey of an American pro golfer of Nepali origin, Binod Thapa, who has played the game in all fifty U.S. states and the seven continents, showcasing his unrelenting passion for the game.

Sridhar Khatri
Ambassador of Nepal to the United States

Golfers all have goals: a great drive that hugs the first cut on that tough par five; the long iron that threads the deep fairway bunkers; that crisp wedge that sticks softly below the hole; and the fifteen-footer that snakes its way to a classic birdie. Most golfers live for those rare journeys on a single hole. But some, like Ben Thapa, chart a course that fulfills a more inspiring journey: a golfer's journey through seven continents and fifty U.S. capitals. It certainly is a story of a love for the game of golf, but more importantly, it is a story of adventure, discovery, friendship, and accomplishment.

Stu Shea
Chairman, President, and Chief Executive Officer, Peraton

Most people have dreams and goals involving travel throughout their lives that mainly never come to fruition. Some of these dreams involve family, friends, activities, and adventures. Few people achieve the journey that Ben Thapa has accomplished by visiting and playing golf in all seven continents and fifty U.S. capitals! He has met many new friends throughout his travels and shared his stories and photos with fellow golfers, family, and friends here at home in South Riding, Virginia. Ben's passion for family, friendship, and golf and his love of travel exceeds all expectations and cannot be matched.

Jon Fulton

Regional Manager, Wingfield Golf

It is my pleasure to read about your journey in the "My Quest for Antarctic Circle" article and your *My Golf Journey* book, which are both educational and entertaining. Both of these show in you the spirit of adventure and courage and exemplify your deep aspiration to earn new knowledge and experiences to make your life worth living as well as to fulfill the dreams you have dreamt and continue dreaming even today.

Professor Damber Bir Thapa

Wow! Congratulations. And to think I was there when you got started.

Jeff Reis

MY GOLF JOURNEY

Across 50 U.S. Capitals
and 7 Continents

Binod "Ben" Thapa

Ballast Books, LLC
www.ballastbooks.com

ISBN: 978-1-962202-37-4

Printed in Hong Kong

Published by Ballast Books
www.ballastbooks.com

For more information, bulk orders, appearances, or speaking requests, please email: info@ballastbooks.com

To my grandparents and parents
who always believed in me and trusted me.

And to all those who welcomed me on
the green along my journey.

Contents

Introduction

Everyone has a special passion or pursuit in their lives. Mine is to travel and play golf. I love nature, so I enjoy playing on vibrant green fairways surrounded by woods and natural beauty. I also gain immense pleasure from traveling around the world, meeting new people, learning about different cultures, and keeping in touch with new friends. Pulling from both of my passions, I had the fortune of completing a lifelong dream of mine. From October 2011 to May 2019, I was able to play golf in all fifty U.S. capitals and in seven continents.

It all started long before that fateful October. I had a college degree in economics from Nepal. But after consulting with an advisor, listening to my wife, Nora, and visualizing the future, I chose to go into the computer field.

We bought our first home in Takoma Park, Maryland, in 1991. It was a fairly small two-story colonial brick house with a beautiful yard. All three of our children—Monica (oldest daughter), AJ (son), and Serena (youngest daughter)—spent the first years of their lives in this home.

For nine years in the 1990s, I used to get up at five in the morning, get ready, and leave for work. I'd take the bus at 6:00 a.m., then hop on the train to Virginia, where the office was located. After work, I would go directly to the university Monday through Thursday for classes. At the time, we had one car, and with kids at home, Nora needed it. But she would drop me off at the bus stop, pick me up at the train station, and drop me off at the university. Then, after class, she would pick me up from there at 10:00 p.m. with the children in the car—a lot of work and effort on her part.

On the weekends, I used to spend a lot of time at the university's library, researching and studying. I spent just as much time at the computer lab for my projects. It definitely was not today's internet era where we could easily take online classes, study, and work on our projects from home. Most of the time—six days a week—I would be out of the house from 6:00 a.m. to 10:30 p.m. for work and for studying. Because English was my second language, I had to study harder than most and spend more time learning English.

Until I graduated, mostly Nora took care of the kids, but since English is her first language, she also advised me on some of my English college projects. With everything else, she also had a part-time job that allowed her to work from home. She was a proposal writer, so most of the time, Nora worked after the kids went to bed late at night. All in all, it was a lot of hard work on both of our parts, but I can say I couldn't have done it without Nora's help. So, to start this book, I must share my deep appreciation and profusely say "thank you!" to Nora!

As we were navigating this crazy schedule, my parents visited us from Nepal for a few months. When they saw we were extremely busy from 6:00 a.m. to 11:00 p.m. every day, my dad said to us, "This is too difficult here in the U.S. In Nepal, we have people working for us at home, cooking, cleaning, and other things. Please move back to Nepal with the family, and we will take care of everything, especially helping with our grandkids."

In response, I told my dad, "Everybody works hard here in the U.S. They cook, clean, and do other things by themselves. In this country, if we work hard and dedicate ourselves to accomplishing our goals, I believe we all can become and achieve anything."

Certainly, I would not have been able to travel and play golf in all fifty U.S. capitals and in seven continents around the world if I had been in Nepal. My life with Nora and my children in the U.S. allowed me to realize my dream.

From 1991 to 1999, when I was working full time and pursuing my undergraduate and graduate degrees, I didn't find much of a chance to play golf regularly. Any time spent outside of work and school was devoted to my family! However, I did manage to play golf in local public courses in Maryland probably seven or eight times a year.

Since my job was located in Virginia, and the commute from our house in Maryland was not easy, we ultimately decided to build a home in South Riding, Virginia. Our family moved there in May 2000.

One of the many reasons I liked this community was because of the South Riding Golf Club (SRGC). I remember visiting the clubhouse a few months after we moved into the community. From the back porch, I saw a beautiful putting green as well as chipping and driving range areas on the back side. To the right, I noted a lovely wooded area from the eighteenth green all the way to the first green, and the ninth hole's putting green looked pristine! But most importantly, the overall view of first, ninth, and eighteenth holes from the back corner of the porch looked stunning! Everything was verdant, and the course looked absolutely beautiful! With a contented sigh, I sat down on the chair there and enjoyed it. Quietly, I said to myself, "I belong here."

All in all, I only played about fifteen rounds per year at SRGC until 2012 because our children were seventeen years old or younger, and we were heavily involved in their sports (football, softball, basketball, soccer, baseball, wrestling) and academic activities. When the kids got older and didn't need us as much as before, I found I had more time to focus on my passion. Nora and the kids knew I would love to play golf more frequently and were supportive of my hobby.

One weekend morning in early 2014, we were having breakfast with the family at home and discussing different things. It was an unusually warm day for that time of the year, and Monica asked "Dad, are you playing golf today? Why don't you join the club and become a member so you can play golf more now that all of us can drive cars?" The rest of the family agreed with Monica's suggestion, so soon after, I became a member at SRGC and started playing regularly. This is how SRGC became my home course!

All three of my children, now adults, graduated from their respective universities, and they currently have jobs and live on their own out of state. There's no doubt they made many sacrifices as I was working and studying during their childhood, and they maintained their support as I pursued this goal of golfing in all U.S. states and all continents on planet Earth. So in addition to my wife, Nora, I would also like to thank Monica, AJ, and Serena for their encouragement on my journey! There are several places I have mentioned them in this book so readers will know who they are and how they have profoundly impacted my life.

Although this book is about my golf adventure across the fifty U.S. capitals and seven continents worldwide, I have also included small stories about my travels relevant to each capital and continent. These travelogues are connected and make my journey more meaningful.

My golf trips were more than just cross-country or international travels. For me, these trips were also helpful in terms of allowing me to understand people and the culture of different regions and countries. During these travels, I met so many wonderful individuals from different places, and I am proud to keep in touch with them to this day. In fact, I have invited many of them here to Washington, D.C., and some of them have already come. This book captures all the salient moments from beginning to end of this incredible adventure that brought together my greatest passions and gave me great pride and fulfillment.

First Time Playing Golf

Believe it or not, before coming to America in 1989, I had never played golf. My first golf game occurred at the Trident Golf Club in Port St. Lucie, Florida, with my father-in-law, Victor, and two brothers-in-law, Jeff and Sandy, in the summer of 1993 during a family reunion.

All of us played with rented clubs. Although I was not terrible, considering it was my first time playing golf, I was still cautious hitting golf balls, especially from the tee box. As a result, Jeff kept telling me, “Grip it and rip it! Whack it!” He was funny and encouraging at the same time. After the round, I thanked Victor, Jeff, and Sandy for bringing me to this golf course. I’d had a wonderful time and discovered a burgeoning love for the sport!

As I mentioned, I am originally from Nepal, and I love nature. So playing on a beautiful golf course, seeing green fairways and trees, was an incredible experience. I just loved being at the golf course and playing the sport for the very first time.

Golfing Across Fifty U.S. Capitals and Seven Continents

It's not easy to play golf in all fifty U.S. capitals and all seven continents across the world, but I took the opportunity to travel and complete this goal over the course of about eight years. Below is a summary of my journey:

Criteria

1) Play golf at U.S. capital golf courses and on each continent
2) Play eighteen holes
3) Play in USGA-rated courses for score-posting purpose
4) Play with the club members or someone local to the area

Motivation

What prompted me to embark on such an incredible journey? I like to stay active, need to have plans, and enjoy working on my checklist items throughout the year, so that likely contributed to my decision to pursue such a lofty goal. My original plan was to play in every state, not necessarily every capital. However, I also wanted to visit all fifty capitol buildings and cities, so I ended up refining my goal accordingly. From there, I decided I wanted to go beyond the U.S. and play across the entire world too! I always wanted to go on cross-country trips, and since I'm from Nepal, I enjoy traveling internationally as well. By playing golf in all fifty capitals and on all seven continents, I would accomplish three things at once: staying active by playing golf, going on cross-country and international trips, and visiting the capital in all fifty states. In the end, I did it!

Logistics

I planned and coordinated these trips over the course of several years. I organized my golf trips by region and traveled alone to all except two capitals—Annapolis and Honolulu. On average, I played golf in four states on each trip. During the fall/winter months, I mostly took trips to southern states, and during the spring/summer, I traveled to northern states.

I always made tee times in two golf courses for the same day. The second tee time was a backup just in case there were some unexpected events at the first golf course. There were a handful of occasions when I had to resort to playing at the second golf course, so it was worth it to have a backup course close by. Also, traveling alone and playing as a single was somewhat beneficial for me. If I missed my tee time, I wouldn't have a problem joining another group. Traveling solo was also beneficial because I could leave the hotel to go to the capitol, explore the area, or leave for the next place anytime I wanted.

That being said, I would definitely like to visit some of these places in the future with my family. It would be wonderful to show them the absolutely amazing scenery and countryside views.

Wherever I played golf in different capitals, after a while, players would ask me why I was there, and I would tell them the story. Usually, they were very curious and interested and admired my goal and journey. I am glad I was able to complete my golf tour!

18/9 Holes

In forty-six capitals, I played at eighteen-hole golf courses. However, Juneau, Alaska; Augusta, Maine; and Montpelier, Vermont had only nine-hole courses, so I had to play twice to make eighteen holes in order to post my scores. Also, in Cheyenne, Wyoming, an eighteen-hole course had an event, so I played in the nine-hole course twice.

Because I had to play in the capital, I didn't want to go outside of the city to play golf in eighteen-hole courses. As we all know, city golf courses typically don't have much land, and they are not as great and beautiful as golf courses in the suburbs. I ended up playing about one-third in municipal golf courses because of my criteria to play golf "only in the capital."

Toward the End

I would say around my thirty-fifth capital, I started to feel that I could truly accomplish my goal. Golf club staff and members were very interested in my journey and extremely welcoming toward me. They would take my picture at the tee box, during lunch at the clubhouse, or at the course. Most of them would have similar comments or ask similar questions. *What a great idea! How did you come up with this unique goal?*

Best Courses

My Favorite Country Clubs:

Honolulu Country Club, Honolulu, HI
Frankfort Country Club, Frankfort, KY
Wolferts Roost Country Club, Albany, NY
Trenton Country Club, Trenton, NJ
Berry Hills Country Club, Charleston, WV
Montpelier Elks Country Club, Montpelier, VT
Concord Country Club, Concord, NH

My Favorite Golf Courses/Clubs:

Hawktree Golf Course, Bismarck, North Dakota
Mendenhall Golf Course, Juneau, Alaska
Fox Ridge Golf Course, Helena, Montana
Silver Oak Golf Course, Carson City, Nevada
Santa Maria Golf Course, Baton Rouge, Louisiana
The Legacy Golf Club, Phoenix, Arizona
Lincoln Park Golf Course, Oklahoma City, Oklahoma
Oak Hills Golf Club, Columbia, South Carolina

Note: Most of these golf courses I noted as "favorite" based on the condition of the course. Some of them I also picked because of the scenery around the golf course, their clubhouses, and the amenities.

Golf Scores

My scores ranged from under par to over my handicap. I would have loved to play better in every golf course in every capital and continent, but I knew it would be a challenge to keep my score lower while trying new courses. Fortunately, I did have some great rounds. Regardless of how I played, I enjoyed all rounds of golf with a great group of people.

$50K SRGC Golf Shirt

I brought our club's white logo golf shirt to all fifty capitals. After playing a round of golf with the players, I would ask them for their autograph. Everybody wrote their name, the course name, the capital and state, and the date we played. This was a very special and valuable shirt for me, and I have framed it to commemorate its meaning. It's not really a $50K golf shirt, but since it is extremely valuable to me, that's what I call it.

Driving Record

Clean! Before I embarked on this journey, I told myself whenever I started driving thousands of miles on these cross-country trips, I also wanted to avoid getting any tickets on the road. When I told Nora about this, she said, "You don't get tickets anyway." Sure enough, I didn't get any tickets, so I was happy.

Souvenirs

As you can see from the pictures included throughout the book, I buy souvenirs everywhere I travel. I have golf shirts, hats, winter clothes, and ball markers with club logos from all fifty capital golf courses. In addition, I buy some other souvenirs from every state and continent—for example, T-shirts, coffee mugs, refrigerator magnets, shot glasses, etc.

Last Capital

Nora is not interested in golf, so she didn't come on any of my trips except for Hawaii. Honolulu was my last capital in which to play golf, so the fact that she accompanied me to Hawaii was special for me.

I played at Honolulu Country Club on Sunday. As we all know, it is not easy to make tee times, especially on the weekend in any country club. I had a little difficulty making the tee time at first, but after I explained why I was in Hawaii to their golf club, they were happy, and I was able to join three other members to play golf. Great people!

This was the best golf course I played in the fifty capitals—probably something to do with scenery. It was also the most expensive course I played, but since I was playing with a great group of people and it was the last golf course, it was worth every bit of it! After I was done playing there, Nora said, "You did it!"

Note: When I was verifying all the capitals, I realized that I had played golf in West Hartford instead of Hartford. So I had to take another trip to play golf in Hartford, Connecticut, in May 2019. That means, officially, Hartford, Connecticut, is my fiftieth capital, not Honolulu, Hawaii. However, because I thought Honolulu was my fiftieth capital, Nora came, and we celebrated. As a result, in my heart, Honolulu is always my fiftieth capital.

Golfing in Each Capital by Region

Although I did ultimately achieve my goal to golf in all fifty U.S. capitals, I didn't do it all at once. I completed this endeavor over the course of several trips, typically visiting multiple capitals in a row before returning home. This portion of the book is organized chronologically with states being grouped together based on when I visited them. Read on to join me on my fifty U.S. capitals golf journey one flight or road trip at a time.

5/25/2017–5/29/2017

Bismarck, North Dakota
Pierre, South Dakota
Cheyenne, Wyoming
Lincoln, Nebraska

North Dakota "Sioux State" – 1st Capital

I had played golf in thirteen states already, but now I was on a new mission and journey—trying to play golf in every U.S. capital. Beginning with a fresh slate and an eager attitude, I was all excited to embark on this adventure. I had been looking forward to visiting North Dakota and playing golf there. There were eight states that I especially wanted to visit, and North Dakota was one of them. So when I landed in Bismarck, I was excited!

When I deboarded the plane, I picked up my golf and carry-on bag and went to the car rental place at the airport in Bismarck. The agent wanted to give me a free upgrade to an SUV, but I declined and asked to get what I had reserved—not that big SUV. The reason is that I feel more comfortable driving midsize cars in unfamiliar areas as opposed to big SUVs—they are much easier to drive around, especially in a new place.

From there, I went to the hotel and checked in. At the Marriott, I received a gift in a bag and an upgraded room. I am a gold elite member and get upgrades without any additional cost in Marriott hotels. Although I was happy to get an upgraded room, I really didn't need it. If I was with my family, it would have been perfect, but I was traveling solo. After taking a shower, I ventured downstairs. At the counter, they gave me some directions on how to get to the golf course.

North Dakota seemed flat in the beginning, but once I started to drive around in the city as well as along the countryside, it was like what I had expected of North Dakota—lots of greenery and lots of mountains.

It was not easy to find the golf course. In fact, I wondered whether the hotel staff may have given me the address of a different golf course because it took me a little while to find my destination.

When I finally arrived, I played one round of golf with three guys at Hawktree Golf Club in Bismarck. They were all members. One of the guys, Fred, was an especially friendly person. He reminded me of another member, Jack, at my own club. Fred introduced me to other members and staff as well as one of the co-owners of the club.

Hawktree was a public but impeccably maintained course that looked semi-private. It reminded me of playing golf in Vermont. The course was beautiful but challenging because of the rolling hills. One of the things I easily remember about this course is the black sand in the bunker. I had never seen this before at a golf course. In one hole, I did hit my golf ball in the sand, and I had a hard time hitting it out because I thought I was hitting from a driveway—an illusion from the black shade of the sand. It almost looked like dark concrete—very strange! All in all, I played fairly well but mostly enjoyed playing with the three players there, particularly Fred. I played with two other guys on the front nine and played with Fred on the back nine.

After the round, I stayed for drinks at the clubhouse. It was kind of on top of the course with glass and looked beautiful looking down below. Fred also introduced me to the GM and staff members. This was my first capital playing golf, so I felt accomplished. I thanked Fred and staff for their hospitality and left the course.

Next, I visited Bismarck and checked out one museum. In the city, I visited the capitol building and a few other places. Even though Bismarck is the capital, the city is not that big. However, it is still a peaceful-looking city!

The next day, outside of the city, I visited Abraham Lincoln State Park in Mandan. There is a lot of history in this place, and it's certainly a beautiful setting! From the top of the tower in Mandan, the panoramic view of North Dakota was breathtaking! I stayed there for a while and enjoyed it immensely! I also bought a few souvenir items from the shop there.

When I drove from North Dakota to South Dakota, there was nothing but cattle ranches by the highway. It was lovely with small green mountains and a stunning view everywhere I looked. There was lush grass, so all the cattle looked big and healthy.

At one point, after four hours of straight driving (that's over 250 miles), I probably saw no more than fifty cars on the highway. There were no police cars and no stores. It was a pretty remote area!

While I was driving along the countryside, I discovered my Garmin GPS was no longer working. I had no 3G reception and no Waze or Google Maps, so I was kind of stuck in one of the crossroads in the middle of nowhere and didn't know which way to go. I waited for about fifteen minutes until another car came to the stop sign. Then, I asked the gentleman for directions. Luckily, I always kept TripTik from AAA and printed out hard copies of my trips just in case. With the directions from the gentleman and additional guidance from the printout, I was able to find the route I was looking for in about thirty minutes.

Golf Course Name:	Hawktree Golf Course
Address and Website:	3400 Burnt Creek Loop, Bismarck, ND 58503 http://hawktree.com/
Capital Players/ Club Contacts:	Fred
Comment:	*"What a surprise it was when I went to Hawktree for the first time since it closed for the season. Never did I expect that they would be holding mail for me. I enjoyed the letter and card and seeing your family. When I saw what it was and who it was from, it made my day special.* *It was good to learn that your U.S. capital tour was such a success. I am sure your journey left you with many stories to share with family and friends. To know that I was part of that journey is special to me. Our round of golf meant much to me. To meet and play golfers such as yourself is part of my journey of getting to know interesting people from different parts of the country as well. I enjoyed our time together, especially when it was spent golfing Hawktree.* *Your invitation, should I ever get to Washington, D.C., is much appreciated. Thanks again for the letter and card. As I said, they were special.* *Oh, by the way, no golf today. Currently, it is -22 degrees F with wind chills expected to get down to -40 to -50 degrees. Fortunately, this too will pass. Hopefully golfing by mid-April. Take care and thanks again. (ND – fs)"*
Highlight:	Although this golf course was a public course, it was nothing like a public course—more like a semi-country club. The rolling hills reminded me of golf courses in Vermont—very pretty! Visiting historic places in Mandan and seeing all around from the top of the small tower was absolutely perfect! I saw cattle farms beside the highway with thick grass and healthy, bulky-looking cattle. In Bismarck and North Dakota, everything looked incredibly pretty!

SOUTH DAKOTA "THE MOUNT RUSHMORE STATE" – 2ND CAPITAL

From Bismarck, North Dakota, to Pierre, South Dakota, is about a three-and-a-half-hour drive that covers 210 miles (US-83 S).

The drive from Bismarck to Pierre was beautiful. These are the mountain states, so what did I expect, right!? There were large cattle farms alongside the highway, gorgeous mountains erupting from the earth, and everywhere I looked, it was all green. Just beautiful!

However, compared to North Dakota, it looked like it was not quite as green. Since I was driving from north to south, the further I traveled, the more I noticed those cattle on the farms didn't look as big and bulky as in North Dakota.

I checked in at the hotel, took a shower, and went downstairs. Then, I headed to the golf course, which was just about a fifteen-minute drive away. This was the only golf course in Pierre.

I checked in at the pro shop but found out there would be nobody to start in the next thirty minutes. So, at first, I started playing alone. Then, I saw another player, but he was going to a different hole. Nonetheless, I walked up to him and introduced myself, asking whether he would be interested in playing with me. He agreed, so I got to enjoy playing golf with Bill at Hillsview Golf Club, the only eighteen-hole golf course in Pierre, South Dakota. Bill was a long hitter. I enjoyed playing the round with him. Afterward, Bill signed my golf shirt and took a couple pictures of me. After he left, I went inside the pro shop and bought a few club logo items.

Before leaving the golf course, I went to the first tee box area to take in the enchanting beauty one more time. I took a few pictures of the course from there. There was also a club restaurant on the left side of the golf course, but I didn't end up dining there.

Next, I visited the capitol building and a few other places while in Pierre. The city is fairly small, but their capitol building is huge with a beautiful dome. I just love capitol domes!

Driving from Pierre to Mount Rushmore and then from Mount Rushmore to Cheyenne took about eight hours total. South Dakota was not as green as North Dakota (I heard because of a drought), so again, those cattle alongside the highway at the ranch didn't look as big and bulky as the cattle in North Dakota. Driving on the highway, there was nothing I could see except cattle on big ranches. There were no houses nearby, and it almost felt like nobody was taking care of the quietly grazing animals.

One thing that occurred to me was, *What happens if there are thunderstorms or lightning, especially because the cattle have nowhere else to go except the open fields?* There were no roofs or other forms of protection. I supposed they might not care too much if they were used to being in the elements.

I was driving for hours and hours on the highway alone and didn't see any people or police cars, which made me think twice. *What happens in an emergency situation in the middle of the highway when there is nobody around—no houses for miles and miles?* I wouldn't be able to get to any stores for help. Fortunately, I didn't have any emergencies.

On one occasion, while driving on the highway, I saw a sign indicating the next service area was in 108 miles. Every eight to ten minutes, I would see cars coming from the opposite direction, but at one point, I didn't see another car coming behind my car for over two hours. It was a very isolated region, but I loved it!

I was at Mount Rushmore for about three hours. There were long lines of cars for the ticket booths. When I was there, it was dark at first, but the sunshine emerged later. I took around a dozen pictures of the monument, and they came out great! I had ice cream and bought a few souvenir items there at the base. There were hundreds of hotels close to the historic site. The area looked very pretty but busy. Overall, Mount Rushmore and the area around it looked absolutely beautiful!

When I stopped at a rest stop on the highway between Pierre and Rapid City, I talked a little bit with two families from Illinois. There was a billboard of South Dakota at the rest stop, and they took their picture in front of it. I also asked them to take my picture, and they were kind enough to oblige. We talked a little bit and then we left. I stopped at Mount Rushmore, which was over one hundred miles away. As I was walking inside Mt. Rushmore, all of a sudden, I saw the same people from the rest stop earlier. We pointed to each other and said, "You again!" It was funny! And, of course, they asked me to take their pictures and they took mine too front of Mt. Rushmore.

Hearing about Standing Rock Indian Reservation and seeing signs for miles and miles before getting there was pretty cool. Then, finally being in that region and actually seeing part of the reservation was special! Also knowing the importance of the Dakota Access Pipeline and finally driving through and crossing felt it seemed enormous. It seemed South Dakota's main attraction was visiting Mount Rushmore, exploring Standing Rock Indian Reservation (ND-SD), and crossing the Dakota Access Pipeline.

Golf Course Name:	Hillsview Golf Course
Address and Website:	4201 SD-34, Pierre, SD 57501 https://www.cityofpierre.org/124/Golf/
Capital Players/ Club Contacts:	Bill R., head pro and manager, and Carin H. and Bryan T.

Comment:	*"Thanks for the picture and the memory of the summer. I enjoyed our conversation and round together. I hope your journey and experiences around the U.S. went well. Have a happy holiday. May your New Year be filled with joy and great experiences."*
Highlight:	Mount Rushmore was astonishingly beautiful! Driving along the countryside for hours and hours looking at the beautiful cattle farms and mountains was unforgettable. I also enjoyed seeing part of Standing Rock Indian Reservation and crossing the Dakota Access Pipeline.

Wyoming "The Cowboy State" – 3rd Capital

From Pierre to Mount Rushmore, South Dakota, to Cheyenne, Wyoming, is about a seven-and-a-half-hour drive covering 460 miles (Routes US-14W, I-90W, US-18W, US-85S).

I always wanted to visit Wyoming, so I was looking forward to this trip to see the countryside and the rest of the state.

Probably one of the best scenic views during the trip was from Mount Rushmore to Wyoming (4.5 hours/270 miles), especially about twenty-five miles before entering Wyoming and another twenty-five miles into the state itself. It was absolutely beautiful driving through the mountains and open fields.

I stopped the car near the border between South Dakota and Wyoming. There was a rest area in both directions on each side of the road, and I parked my car on the Wyoming side. It was a pretty-looking area from both angles. There were other people who had also stopped their cars and were taking pictures from there. I took several pictures myself that included the "Welcome to Wyoming" on one side and "Welcome to South Dakota" on the other. I was happy to be in Wyoming!

Then, I drove directly to the hotel in Cheyenne. This was one of Marriott's property hotels. It was located at the border of the city, and there were a couple of other hotels nearby. When I arrived, I checked in and went to my room as usual. After showering, I went downstairs and asked the receptionist at the counter for a restaurant recommendation in the city. They gave me the name of a restaurant that was just about a five- to seven-minute drive from the hotel.

At the restaurant, I ordered roasted pork ribs. Although I was tired and not hungry, the pork was really tasty, so I couldn't help but enjoy it! After dinner, I returned to the hotel to rest.

Cheyenne and the surrounding areas were bigger than Bismarck and Pierre, or at least that's how it felt. The next morning, I visited my usual places in the capital: the capitol building, museums, and other historic places. It was a beautiful and sunny day. The capitol dome and that section of the city looked very pretty. Next to the small museum, there was a seven- to eight-foot-tall cowboy boot. That boot looked really unique because of its size and color and how shiny it was! I took a couple of pictures.

Initially, I had a tee time at two different golf courses. When I arrived at the first one, they had a tournament, so I couldn't start for another two hours. Then, I drove to Prairie View Golf Course, which was my backup course, where I played golf with Ken and two other guys. Although the course was public, it was still pretty! Ken and the other two guys were pleasant, and I enjoyed playing with them. Later, we took a group picture. All three of them signed my golf shirt and left right after playing nine holes. Since this was a nine-hole course, I had to play another nine holes to reach eighteen. To my delight, I played really well at this course.

For some reason, I completely forgot to ask Ken and the other two guys for their phone numbers. Luckily, after I contacted the golf course a few months later, they found another golfer named Ken who also regularly played golf at that course, and we exchanged multiple text messages. The other Ken (who was very helpful) found the original Ken B. whom I had played golf with. I was grateful to reconnect with my golf pal!

Driving through the countryside, I, of course, could see nothing but cattle ranches again. There were a few times when I noticed that some of the cattle were walking much differently than the rest. Later, I realized that one or two of those in the herd were young buffalo. They had probably been separated from their parents and the rest of their buffalo herd and ended up with the cattle instead. I felt sorry for them.

As I was driving through the Dakotas and Wyoming for hundreds of miles and seeing all those ranches, only once did I see two guys on horses heading toward the cattle. While I was playing golf with Ken, I even asked him whether anybody would take care of these roaming cattle. He responded, "No, people own different ranches with hundreds to thousands of acres of land. The owners go and see the cattle every once in a while." Interesting—I didn't know that!

Overall, I enjoyed the nature and the beauty of Wyoming!

Golf Course Name:	Prairie View Golf Course
Address and Website:	3601 Windmill Rd., Cheyenne, WY http://airportgolfclub.com/
Capital Players/ Club Contacts:	Ken B. and Ken V.

Comment:	*"I will keep you updated. Prairie View is like my home course, so it shouldn't be too hard to find him. I will find him. This is going to be fun! I found out that his name is Ken B., and his number is 307-635-xxxx. Chris told me about your mission to play golf in every capital city in the U.S. It sounds like you like to golf as much as I do."*
Highlight:	Seeing the mountains of Wyoming, driving on highways with beautiful views all around for miles and miles, and being able to play golf there with great people were all special! Since Wyoming was one of the states that I most wanted to visit and everything went as planned, I was thrilled!

Nebraska "The Cornhusker State" – 4th Capital

From Cheyenne, Wyoming, to Lincoln, Nebraska, is about a six-and-a-half-hour drive covering 440 miles (Route I-80 E).

From Cheyenne, after just a few miles going south, the road merged onto Route 80 East. I didn't see any welcome state sign, but after driving for a while, I realized I was already in Nebraska because I started to see many vehicles on this part of Route 80—and it was not as isolated as in Wyoming. I could see cars, trucks, service areas, and stores everywhere now. In fact, I spotted more trucks on Route 80 than cars. It seemed trucks owned this part of Route 80.

Along the highway in Nebraska, I stopped a couple of times at rest stops and at a gas station. I saw two different signs that I thought were funny: "Pet Exercise Area" at a rest stop and "Free Wireless Internet" at a hotel. I had seen pet walking areas before but not exercise areas. Also, these days, I thought internet is typically free at any hotel, so "Free Wireless Internet" made me smile.

When I drove by Kearney, Nebraska, I kind of felt like I knew this place. We used to have some family members who went to the university and lived there. So when I passed through, I *really* felt like I was in Nebraska, even though I obviously had been for a while.

It was a very long drive to get to Lincoln. I parked at the Marriott lot late in the evening and texted Nora to let her know I had arrived. The hotel restaurant was already closed, and I didn't feel like going out to eat, so I ordered some Chinese food.

The next morning, I went downtown to explore the capital. Nebraska's capitol building was totally different. It was very tall with just a small dome on the top. It was a unique-looking capitol but beautiful! The campus was also gorgeous. After that, I went to the University of Nebraska and took a tour of the city.

I played golf on the front nine with Jim and his son at Highlands Golf Course in Lincoln. The golf course advertised Marriott on one of the tee boxes, so it felt familiar. While there, I also took a picture with Jim.

On the back nine, I played with another gentleman who was very friendly! I played better during the second half. Overall, the course was very well-maintained.

My golf trip across this region ended fairly well and went almost exactly as planned. I enjoyed my trip!

Golf Course Name:	Highlands Golf Course (Lincoln City Golf)
Address and Website:	5501 NW 12th St., Lincoln, NE 68521 http://lincolncitygolf.org/
Capital Players/ Club Contacts:	Jim M. and son (members)
Comment:	*"Happy to hear that you are trying this!"*

Highlight:	There are many Nepalese students that go to universities in Nebraska, including a few from our families. I believe most of them went to Kearney, so passing through there reminded me of our families and other Nepalese students. It felt like I had a connection with the state of Nebraska.

6/24/2017

Harrisburg, Pennsylvania

Pennsylvania "Keystone State" – 5th Capital

From South Riding, Virginia, to Harrisburg, Pennsylvania, is about a two-hour drive covering 110 miles (Route US-15 N).

One early morning in June, I drove to Harrisburg, Pennsylvania, to play one round of golf there. Harrisburg is very close to Dickinson College in Carlisle, Pennsylvania, where Monica attended. But instead of making a left on Route 74 from Route 15, I would have to go straight on Route 15 and a little further north.

I had called this golf course a few days in advance to make a tee time, but they had suggested, for a single player, just to come to the clubhouse, and they would try to pair me up with other groups. I still didn't want to take a chance, so I called Golf Now and arranged the tee time before getting there.

I played at Dauphin Highlands Golf Course with Cord (who is a member there), Bill, and Douglas. The course was actually very nice—not too flat or too hilly. It was a good combination. The three guys were kind and fairly decent players. Bill and Douglas were complimentary of my game. However, it seemed Cord was trying a little too hard, and often when you do that in golf, you make more mistakes. As a result, Cord kept telling Bill and Douglas that he was not playing well that day. Douglas said he agreed that he was not playing up to his usual standard, but Doug also jokingly added, "Playing with Ben doesn't help you either." What he meant was that I was hitting the ball straight and not missing much, and that puts pressure on other players. In response, Cord smiled. We all knew what Doug was talking about.

But it is golf—sometimes we have good days, and sometimes we have bad days. That's just what happens in golf!

All in all, I enjoyed playing with those guys! At the end, Cord signed my golf shirt. I also bought a club logo shirt, a hat, and a few other things at the pro shop. I stayed a little longer and talked to a few guys at the club before finally leaving. The two-and-a-half-hour drive back home on Route 15 South was just fine because I had driven a number of times on this road, and it didn't feel like I was traveling out of state. It was a pleasant drive after a pleasant day of golf.

Golf Course Name:	Dauphin Highlands Golf Course
Address and Website:	650 S Harrisburg St., Harrisburg, PA 17113 https://www.golfdauphinhighlands.com/
Capital Players/ Club Contacts:	Cord H., Bill B., and Douglas S.
Comment:	*"I am happy that we were able to be part of your journey. I personally may take you up on your offer of golf in May. I'm going to be driving to South Carolina, and if I can stop and break up the trip with golf, I will do it. If you are ever back up this way, let me know because I'm always looking at getting out. I have forwarded this email to my brother-in-law Bill and our buddy Douglas."*
Highlight:	It was a sunny day, and the course looked beautiful! Playing with Cord, Bill, and Douglas was enjoyable!

6/29/2017–7/4/2017

Juneau, Alaska
Olympia, Washington
Salem, Oregon
Boise, Idaho
Helena, Montana

Alaska "The Last Frontier State" – 6th Capital

Alaska was always on the top of my bucket list. If I had to choose one state to visit, I would have always picked Alaska before and even now. Probably because Alaska is like Nepal with big mountains and greenery. It's a great place to live if you like nature. In addition, Alaska is up north, so being closer to the Arctic Circle probably has something to do with my love for it as well.

When I visited Juneau, Alaska, the problem was that there was no Marriott, so I stayed at The Alaskan Hotel & Bar instead. It was in a great location downtown. I took the tram to go up Mount Roberts, which was great. I could see a beautiful view down below Juneau next to the river. Up in the mountains, there were multiple hiking trails. I went on one of those trails, enjoying a pleasant nature walk with beautiful scenery. While strolling, I noticed a lot of wildflowers everywhere on the mountains, which made it look even prettier. I also spotted a bald eagle, something I had never seen up close before.

The city of Juneau has about thirty thousand people in total. Juneau also has a port for big ships. When I was there, there were three huge ships docked. When I say huge, I mean they were tremendously big. On these three ships, there were more people than in the entire city of Juneau.

I usually research places before I actually visit there. One of the things I had looked up about Juneau was the average temperature in the months of June and July. According to my research, the average temperature was sixty-eight degrees in that time frame. So I was thinking about not taking a single pair of pants on the trip; I only wanted to bring shorts. Then, I said to myself, *Let me take at least one pair of golf pants.* In the end, I was glad I did. When I was leaving to go to Mendenhall Glacier in the morning, it was about forty degrees. This was a very low temperature for the middle of the summer, but after all, it was Alaska.

I took a delightful tour of the Mendenhall Glacier area and walked around the trail. In the middle, I could see a tremendous glacier. There was a waterfall on the right and an open area with a beautiful view on the left. Absolutely gorgeous! I also met a mother and daughter from Phoenix, Arizona, there at the glacier. When we were talking, I found out that the daughter had traveled to Nepal in 1980. They were very happy to talk to me, and I was happy to talk to them too. They had come to Juneau on one of those big ships.

Next on the agenda was a tour of the Alaska state capitol building. Most capitol buildings have domes, but not Alaska's. Inside the capitol building in Juneau, I had the opportunity to check out some historic memorabilia items, which I enjoyed seeing. Downtown Juneau is not that big, but it's very pretty situated by the water. Since I was staying in the middle of downtown, it was convenient for me to get wherever I needed to go. The boardwalk by the water was a lot of fun as well.

Juneau has only one par-three nine-hole golf course—Mendenhall Golf Course. I played there with Brian and Brad. Since it was only a nine-hole course, I had to play twice to make one complete round. Their putting green was like the first cut (rather rough as opposed to smooth putting green), and I was not used to it. As a result, it took me a couple of holes to figure it out. But when I played the second time for another nine holes, it was much easier.

Dan was the owner of this golf course. He said his grandparents started the business, and he kept the course running.

It was not crystal clear the day I played golf, but the weather was great. The Mendenhall Glacier side was not super visible, but I could still see the glacier a little bit from the golf course. It was a breathtaking view. I felt lucky to be able to play golf in Alaska just below the Mendenhall Glacier.

Brian and Brad were very funny and friendly people. I enjoyed playing with them. Before they left, they wished me good luck on the golf journey. I spoke to Dan, who was helpful and engaging, for a little bit after the game and then bought some golf souvenirs from the golf shop.

I use GoPro whenever I travel cross-country. This is a small, portable video recorder that can also be used for pictures with advanced features. As you can probably imagine, I used GoPro multiple times in Alaska to capture the beautiful nature and scenery.

It was kind of strange to experience nighttime in Alaska at that time of year. It was only dark at night for about three and a half hours. From 2:30 a.m. to 11:00 p.m., it was daylight. I had a little trouble sleeping at night because of how bright it was and because of the four-hour time difference from Washington, D.C., to Juneau—jet lag.

I had rented a car at the airport, so it was easy for me to visit places I wanted to explore. I enjoyed Juneau, Alaska, very much. Every place I visited in that city was just gorgeous, and people were very friendly. The elevation of Alaska is pretty high, so it reminded me of trekking in the mountains in the northern part of Nepal. I know we will visit Alaska in the future again. I left Juneau, Alaska, with a great impression and memory that I will never forget.

Golf Course Name:	Mendenhall Golf Course
Address and Website:	2101 Industrial Blvd, Juneau, AK 99801 (No website)
Capital Players/ Club Contacts:	Brian S., Brad K., Dan (Owner)
Comment:	*"You are trying to play in all fifty capitals, which is great. Safe travels!"*
Highlight:	The view of Mendenhall Glacier from the golf course was just gorgeous! Seeing over twenty hours of daylight was incredible as well.

WASHINGTON "EVERGREEN STATE" – 7TH CAPITAL

When traveling, I usually rent a car at the airport and drive to the hotel first to check in. According to my online research, renting a car at the Seattle airport versus renting a car in the city was almost five hundred dollars more. So I booked the car in the city. After I arrived in Seattle from Juneau, I took the city train and then the bus to get to this rental place downtown. I had my golf bag and carry-on, along with my backpack, so it was not easy to transfer from the train, walk to the bus stop, and eventually get to the rental location. It was about twenty-five miles from the airport, but it felt like it took forever. Finally, when I arrived and got the car, I felt much better, particularly since I saved five-hundred dollars.

First, I drove downtown to the Space Needle and parked nearby. The tower looked spectacular, especially since it was a sunny day. I walked around a little bit from there. I also wanted to visit the Major League Baseball (MLB) park and National Football League (NFL) stadium. Because of traffic, I missed one exit, so it took me forever to get back to CenturyLink Field (Seattle Seahawks) and Safeco Field (Seattle Mariners). Both stadiums were very close to each other. I parked a few blocks away and walked from there. As I strolled along, I saw big banners of some of the players hanging on the wall. What an impressive sight!

In the afternoon, I drove from Seattle to Olympia. Because of the Friday traffic, it took me much longer than expected, so I needed to change some of my plans. Since the capitol building was on the way to the hotel, I stopped there first. There were a lot of legislators present, and they appeared to be very busy. I found out from one of them that they were trying to pass the budget by midnight; otherwise, the city (government buildings, parks, etc.) would be shut down. I thought this kind of problem only happened in Washington, D.C., but I guess it can happen in Washington state too!

There was a pond on the right side of the building, so I walked around there for a bit. Out of all of the state capitol buildings, Olympia's was probably the biggest and prettiest I had seen at that point. The capitol building, along with the surrounding area, was just beautiful!

One thing I realized is that most of the Marriotts on the West Coast don't have room service or restaurants open late at night. Luckily, I arrived early enough to enjoy a meal out. At this location specifically, they recommended that I go to one of their special restaurants by the water. It was a beautiful place. I enjoyed the seafood and the setting overall.

When I came back to the hotel, the receptionist asked me how the food had been at the restaurant. Obviously, I said it was great and thanked her for recommending it. But on the inside, I kind of wanted to tell her that although my Marriott status was gold, they could treat me as if I had silver status. When I was on these kinds of trips, I didn't have two to three hours to sit down at a restaurant and eat three-course meals, especially since I was not with my family. Time was more precious for me on those occasions. Regardless, I enjoyed the great food and the atmosphere in the restaurant by the water.

The next morning, I went to play golf at the Capitol City Golf Club in Olympia. I found three guys, Richard, Tony, and Justin, to play golf with. I enjoy talking to other people while playing, as golfers are usually very polite and respectful. When they saw I was playing well and not missing much with my shots, Tony said to his friends, "This is why Ben travels to play golf." The course was pretty decent, and there were a couple of beautiful holes.

After our round, Richard, Tony, and Justin signed my golf shirt. Tony also took a couple of pictures of me. Then, on the highway on the way to Oregon, I found a local gift shop where I bought T-shirts, a coffee mug, and a few other things. I was glad to have some souvenirs from this leg of the trip.

Golf Course Name:	Capitol City Golf Club
Address and Website:	5225 Yelm Hwy SE, Olympia, WA http://www.golfcapitolcity.com/
Capital Players/ Club Contacts:	Richard, Tony, Justin
Comment:	*"You hit straight, and your chipping and putting is very good . . . that's why Ben travels around to play golf."*

Highlight:	Visiting the NFL and MLB stadiums in Seattle. Seeing the beautiful capitol building and campus with pretty flowers. I also enjoyed walking around the pond area that had great gardens and landscaping a little further down the hill. Last but not least, I enjoyed the three-course dinner at a lovely restaurant looking at the view of the pond.

Oregon "Beaver State" – 8th Capital

The distance between Olympia, Washington, and Boring, Oregon, is about a two-hour drive covering 130 miles (Route I-5 S).

Because I hit bad traffic the day before when traveling from Seattle to Olympia, I was about four hours, or half a day, behind schedule on my trip. I was supposed to leave Olympia first thing Saturday morning, but instead, I left around 1 p.m.

Driving from Olympia, Washington, to Boring, Oregon, was pretty. I arrived at the home of Nora's brother and sister-in-law in Boring, Oregon, late afternoon. Once I arrived, I let them know why I was late and apologized.

It was great to see Jeff and Sarah and their son, our nephew, Forest. They knew I wanted to play golf, so soon after I arrived, Jeff, Forest, and I went to Mountain View Golf Course nearby, where we played nine holes. Jeff played especially well from the same blue tee box as me. Forest also held his own. I told him if he could play regularly and on different courses, he could become a strong golfer.

I had a fairly decent round myself. I had a couple of birdies, but mostly pars. Jeff referred to me as a scratch golfer, meaning a golfer with zero handicap. I know I am not a scratch player, but it was a kind compliment, especially because Jeff was the first one who taught me how to play golf.

Afterward, we went back to their home. Jeff had built that house over twenty-five years previously with some help from family and friends. It was a beautiful house, and it is special because they ordered all of the materials and built it themselves. I believe it took them over a year to finish. Jeff and his family should be proud of this tremendous accomplishment!

They have two acres of land, along with a colorful and attractive vegetable garden. They also have seven different pets at home. I had a pleasant dinner with them. After the meal, we sat down in the living room and talked a little bit while watching some TV. I also showed Jeff my golf shirt with autographs from players from different capitals. Jeff added his own signature!

Their place was very enjoyable and low key. When I went to bed, the window was open, allowing a fresh breeze to waft inside. I slept soundly through the night. Usually, I wake up very easily because I sleep so lightly, but not this time.

Early the next morning, I had a tasty breakfast. Then, I let Jeff and Sarah know that I'd had a great time and that it was good to see the family. Finally, I said thank you and left their house.

From there, I drove to Salem, which was about one hour away. After driving around the city, I went to the capitol building. It was obviously smaller, but the area was similar to D.C. There was even a reflecting pool, and it was a beautiful area!

From downtown, I went to the Salem Golf Club and played there with Randy and Linda, an older retired couple who were members at the club. They were very polite. I had a stimulating conversation with them. Before I left, I asked for their autographs for my golf shirt. They said no one had ever asked them for their autographs before, so they were happy to oblige.

Whenever I play golf in different capitals, I like to play with local people and capture their signatures with the club's name, the state and capital, and the date. After the round, I changed into travel clothes inside the members' bathroom. Then, before I left, I bought a golf course shirt, hat, logo ball, ball marker, etc., at the clubhouse.

After leaving the golf course, I headed toward Boise, Idaho. The first two hours of the drive from Portland, Oregon, were absolutely breathtaking! I was driving on I-84 East alongside the Columbia/Snake River. On the right side, I had a lovely view of the mountains. On the left side, I could see a clear blue river and freight trains passing slowly every thirty minutes or so. There were beautiful towns and cities and thousands of windmills on the right side, which was absolutely gorgeous! This was the kind place where I could see myself retiring—except it was in the north, and there were not a lot of golf courses around there!

Golf Course Name:	Salem Golf Club
Address and Website:	18 Bloomer Rd., North Salem, NY 10560 https://salemgolfclub.com/
Capital Players/ Club Contacts:	Randy and Linda
Comment:	*"Good luck with your travel. It was great meeting you!"*
Highlight:	It was great to see Jeff and his family in Oregon. Jeff, Forest, and I played nine holes of golf at Mountain View Golf Club, which was great! I had a delicious dinner at Jeff's house, enjoyed great conversations, and spent the night sleeping soundly on the upper floor with the windows open.

Idaho "Gem State" – 9th Capital

From Salem, Oregon, to Boise, Idaho, it is about a nine-hour and 475-mile drive (Route I-84 East).

In different parts of Idaho, I passed many open and dry fields. In fact, for a while, I saw miles and miles of farms with ripened golden crops. When I saw these beautiful yellow crops, I thought about those stunning photos at Nora's parents' house. I believe they bought them in Boise, Idaho, while they were visiting Nora's sister Fran.

Idaho had scenic views alongside the road up in the higher areas. Then, the views from the mountain below were gorgeous! Some parts of the highways were kind of isolated, but not as isolated as a few of the other states that I had been to.

It was a long but absolutely beautiful drive to Boise. Once there, I stayed at a Marriott downtown where I had dinner and went to bed early.

While I was in Idaho, I visited a few places. The University of Idaho was across from the hotel, and I especially wanted to see the Broncos stadium with its unique blue and orange field. I also visited the capitol building and walked around downtown in the morning.

In addition to exploring the capitol and other historic places, I usually like to try authentic/signature foods from the places I visit. As we all know, Idaho is famous for potatoes. I was not really interested in a main course potato dish, but I did have potatoes as a side.

Next, I played golf with Roger and Rob at Boise Ranch Golf Course. They were very engaging and funny, which made the round even more enjoyable. I had a wonderful time with them. Most of the course was fairly flat, but a few holes were a bit higher. It was a decent course overall.

That particular day, it was almost one hundred degrees. When I play in hot weather like that, I usually drink a lot of water to stay hydrated.

After the round, I stayed at the clubhouse and had lunch with Roger and Rob. We all enjoyed a pleasant chat. Then, I bought a few golf shirts, hats, and markers with the course logo from the pro shop before leaving.

During the drive from Boise to Helena, Montana, while still driving in Idaho, at one point, I was supposed to turn left, but I accidentally passed the exit. It was about eight to ten miles before I could find another exit to turn around. Obviously, this was my first time in Idaho, and everything looked new, so there was nothing I could recognize. However, after driving in Idaho's countryside for hours in an isolated area, where nothing looked familiar, I abruptly spotted a Walmart truck. Believe it or not, it felt good to spot something so familiar. I chuckled to myself that I recognized something even in this part of the region.

I kept driving north and couldn't see much from the highway. I still had a third of a tank of gas, but I didn't want to risk running out. So I took the first exit I saw with a gas sign and filled up. Later, as I was driving, one Hispanic family pointed toward my car hood; it was a little open, and I didn't realize. At the gas station, I had tried to open the gas cap, but I must have opened the hood instead by mistake. I was happy they saw and mentioned the open hood. I was also pleased to see people from Central and South America in this region. (The U.S. attracts a lot of temporary seasonal workers for farming from Central/South America, especially in that region.)

From there, I took the ramp to get onto the highway. As soon as I got on the highway, I looked to the left and saw a beautiful golf course and neighborhood. I couldn't believe this! There was nothing else around. It was kind of a deserted area, yet there was this nice golf course. I had my clubs in the car, and I could have stayed and played, but everything was scheduled for me, so I didn't have time.

In Idaho, I saw a few dams, and I also spotted thousands of pretty windmills on the road—very impressive! I also passed Idaho Falls alongside the highway. I wanted to stop there, but I didn't have time, so I kept on heading toward Helena, Montana.

Golf Course Name:	Boise Ranch Golf Course
Address and Website:	6501 S Cloverdale Rd., Boise, ID 83709 http://www.boiseranchgc.com/
Capital Players/ Club Contacts:	Roger C. and Rob H.
Comment:	*"Ben, I'm glad you are doing this. You completed seven continents, and you are trying to finish fifty capitals. What's your next plan . . . the moon?" Then, he smiled.*
Highlight:	Seeing miles and miles of beautiful farms and open fields in Idaho. Spotting a Walmart truck in an area that was completely unfamiliar. Noting a beautiful golf course and neighborhood in an otherwise deserted area.

MONTANA "BIG SKY/TREASURE STATE" – 10TH CAPITAL

The trip from Boise, Idaho, to Helena, Montana, is about an eight-hour and 480-mile drive (Routes 20-E and I-15N).

I always wanted to visit Montana—maybe because it is in the north, because it is mountainous, or because I've seen documentaries/movies on Montana. But perhaps it could be because Rajan and Manoj—my best friend and cousin—went to college in Miles City, Montana, for the first two years. That's how they started their journey, and they created a lot of memorable stories in the state. So I always relate Montana with them.

From Idaho, I was heading north toward Montana. I could have gone a totally different route from Boise to Helena because the distance was much shorter. But even though this route was much longer, it would take about the same amount of time or possibly even less on the highway. Also, my Garmin didn't want to take me on the smaller roads. I likely would have seen even more scenic views if I had gone on the smaller highways, but sometimes, it's better to take major highways if you are new or unfamiliar with the area.

I would say about twenty to thirty miles before getting to Montana, I could feel that I was getting closer to the state. I started seeing beautiful red mountains and just bare ones like in Tibet. Because it was very cold, there were not many trees on the mountains. If there were any, there were only smaller ones.

As you can probably imagine, driving in Montana was isolated but quite pretty. I could see a few trucks and cars but not that many on the road. Everything seemed new and strange. When I saw a U.S. postal truck on the road, I felt like I finally recognized something familiar.

On the way to Helena, I saw Butte City, where I took in an absolutely beautiful view from the nearby scenic area. It was getting darker, and I still needed to drive for more than an hour, so I didn't linger long.

In this section of the highway, there were ten to twelve miles of road construction in very dangerous areas with mountains and narrow roads creating additional hazards. At one point, I saw a sign saying "drive carefully—twelve people have lost control and died" or something of that nature. I know they say there is no speed limit in Montana. On the one hand, they had this sign; on the other hand, there was a speed limit of eighty miles per hour on that narrow and dangerous road. I started thinking to myself, *Why not forty or forty-five miles per hour as the speed limit to save lives?*

Helena is beautiful. From the Marriott, I could see the magnificent valley below. In the morning, I went to the capitol building area first. The dome and campus with lovely flowers looked gorgeous! Helena is not very big and crowded, but the city is below mountains and expands into the valley. It was beautiful and peaceful!

From the city, I went to Fox Ridge Golf Course in Helena, Montana. I had called and made the tee time at this public course about two weeks prior. When I arrived, I introduced myself to Helen at the pro shop. I also let her know that I had come to play at their course as part of my capital tour. She was happy that I'd picked their course.

Helen, who was a super friendly person, said she would like to pair me up with Bill. According to her, Bill worked at this golf club part time once a week and was a decent golfer. That's exactly who I needed to play with! Helen asked me to wait to play with Bill so he could show me the course. Gladly, I waited.

Bill was a very polite person. We played together, and he graciously showed me the course. It was pretty for a public course, but most notably, the view of the mountains and valley with flowers looked magnificent!

We took a few selfies, then Bill also said he would take some pictures of me at the course. At the turn (in golf, when nine holes have been finished and you're making the turn at the clubhouse before starting the back nine), we stopped at the pro shop for water. Helen asked Bill, "Are you showing our course to Ben?" Then, Bill wittily responded, "Actually, Ben is showing me the course" (meaning playing better). That was funny!

I guess a couple of years ago, a mother fox had given birth to a baby fox at the course and raised the baby there. Everybody talked about that, and Jim H., another member, texted me a few pictures a few days later. Usually, wild animals don't like to be near people, let alone raise their babies in a neighborhood where there are a lot of people. I guess this was an exception!

I bought a golf shirt and a hat from the pro shop. Since the shop didn't have a logo golf ball, Jim gave me a used GC logo ball. That was kind of him!

From Helena, I drove to Great Falls, which was about an hour and a half and ninety miles away on I-15 North. I stopped one more time at a rest stop/scenic view area to take a look at the gorgeous mountains and valley. Great Falls is a beautiful city. I bought a few souvenirs before returning the car at the airport and entering the terminal.

This was an amazing trip but probably the hardest one in terms of driving from one state to another on small roads and through the mountains. Nonetheless, I enjoyed seeing different parts of the country, driving, and meeting people!

I texted a few pictures of Montana to Rajan and Manoj while I was in Helena, letting them know that I was in their state. I enjoyed exchanging a few text messages with them.

Golf Course Name:	Fox Ridge Golf Course
Address and Website:	4020 Lake Helena Drive, Helena, Montana 59602 https://foxridgegolfcourse.com/
Capital Players/ Club Contacts:	Dave F., Jim U., and Pro Shop Helen

Comment:	*"Thanks for choosing our course for your journey. It was a pleasure playing with you."*
Highlight:	Seeing gorgeous mountains of Montana. There were a few states I particularly wanted to visit, and Montana was one of them. Coming from Nepal, I always liked mountains and nature.

7/22/2017

Richmond, Virginia

Virginia "The Old Dominion State" – 11th Capital

From South Riding to Richmond, Virginia, is about a two-and-a-half-hour drive covering 120 miles (Route I-95 S).

I drove to Glenwood Golf Club in Richmond, Virginia, on one hot day in July. I have driven to Richmond and back many times because I used to take my family members there.

Glenwood Golf Course is a public course, and it has a fairly decent rate. I played the first nine holes with Pete, a member at this club. He only wanted to play nine holes, so after finishing them, we sat down outside on a bench and talked for about half an hour.

After Pete left, I started to play the back nine alone. In the middle of the day, the actual temperature was ninety-six degrees, and the heat index was 103. This was probably the hottest weather that I'd played golf in that year. Normally, when golfers start playing, they focus on hitting their next shot, improving, and beating their opponents, etc. They do not fixate much on the weather. After all, they typically can play in most weather conditions. I am no different, but I did take note of the heat that day!

I caught up with another gentleman, John, on hole eleven, and we played the rest of the back nine together. I hit my first 304-yard drive on one of the holes on the back side at this course. It was my first 300+ yard drive, so I saved the golf ball. I did fairly well and enjoyed playing with John. His kids were similar ages to Monica and AJ, so besides talking about golf, we spoke about their college experiences and a few other things.

After the game, I bought a logo hat (they didn't have a golf shirt) and a few other items and left. But I also stopped at the capitol building in downtown Richmond before heading back home.

Incidentally, I had to drive to Richmond twice because I forgot to get my golf shirt signed when I played there the first time. I was happy that it happened in Virginia and not in Alaska or Hawaii!

Golf Course Name:	Glenwood Golf Club
Address and Website:	3100 Creighton Rd., Richmond, VA 23223 https://stpaul.golf/highland-national-gc/
Capital Players/ Club Contacts:	Pete T., Jimmy B., Staff Cliff S.
Comment:	*"The pleasure was mine, and I am still telling people how interesting you were and that it was a nice afternoon of golf."*
Highlight:	I was playing with John at Glenwood Golf Course in Richmond on the back nine. It was either on hole twelve or thirteen that I drove 304 yards. John looked at me, smiled, and said, "Great drive!" That was my first 300+ drive! It felt good, and I saved the golf ball.

9/1/2017–9/4/2017

St. Paul, Minnesota
Madison, Wisconsin
Des Moines, Iowa
Springfield, Illinois

Minnesota "North Star State" – 12th Capital

I had flown to Minneapolis a few times before. Every time the plane approaches the MSP airport, I love seeing the view of Minnesota below from the plane. Houses are well-maintained, communities are well-designed, it is all green and white, and those ten thousand lakes make everything beautiful there. Probably besides Alaska, Minnesota is the second best state I have seen so far for the great aerial view.

I played one round of golf at Highland National Golf Course in St. Paul. I played the front nine with Dan and Lynn, a father and son duo—very polite people! Then, I played with three members: Greg, Joel, and Brian. They were all very good golfers, especially Greg. He was a better golfer, as he had four birdies in nine holes. I also played fairly well and hit long balls, so after a couple of holes, they realized I was a strong golfer and started complimenting my game as well. I enjoyed playing all of them.

After the round, my cousin Chetan and I went inside the pro shop, where I bought a few golf club logo items.

While in Minnesota, I stayed with my cousin Chetan, who lives in Minneapolis. We also went to visit the state capitol building as well as the MLB and NFL stadiums. We went to the state capitol building in St. Paul first. It was on a separate side of the city. The dome and the campus looked very pretty in the morning sun. I love Midwest and mountain states' capitols . . . they are big, well-designed, and beautiful!

When I came to the U.S, I didn't know much about baseball or American football at first. But I remember I started watching these sports in 1990. In 1991, the Minnesota Twins won the World Series, and I clearly remember Kirby Puckett. He was a small and stocky player but a very powerful and impressive player. He is a Hall of Famer now. Because I had started watching baseball around the time the Twins won the World Series, I always remember the Minnesota Twins as a notable team. As a result, visiting the Twins baseball park was special!

Chetan gave me a few golf items in Minnesota. One of them was a long sleeve gray golf shirt for mild winter. Actually, I needed that . . . and I continue to wear that golf shirt frequently when I play golf.

Golf Course Name:	Highland National Golf Course
Address and Website:	1403 Montreal Avenue, St. Paul, MN 55116 https://stpaul.golf/
Capital Players/ Club Contacts:	Dan and Lynn E., Greg, Joel, Brian
Comment:	*"Hitting straight in the middle every time. Good to hear you are planning to play at all fifty capitals."*
Highlight:	I hadn't seen Chetan in years, so seeing him and spending a couple of days with him was my highlight in Minnesota.

WISCONSIN "THE DAIRY STATE" – 13TH CAPITAL

From Minneapolis, Minnesota, to Green Bay to Milwaukee to Madison, Wisconsin, is about eight hours and 480 miles (Routes I-94E, WI-29E, I-43S, I-94W).

Driving from Minneapolis to Green Bay (four and a half hours/280 miles) was less exciting than what I had expected. There was a lot of construction and no scenic views. I was expecting to see great farmland and lots of red colored silos from the highway, but I didn't see much. Some of the silos were not even red, so I was kind of disappointed.

My first stop in Wisconsin was in Green Bay. I went to Lambeau Field, and I enjoyed taking pictures in front of the Vince Lombardi statue there. Most sports fans know that Lombardi was a player and coach and that the Super Bowl trophy was named after him. He is a very popular coach and household name when it comes to American football. I wanted to buy an Aaron Rodgers jersey for AJ from the stadium there, but most of their gift shops were already closed, so I couldn't buy one. Overall, it was a great stadium!

From there, I drove around the city. Then, I walked around a little bit and had dinner. The Marriott downtown was a beautiful building.

The next morning, from Green Bay, I drove to Milwaukee (about two hours/120 miles). I parked in the city and saw a few sights, but mostly, I was interested in going to see the Milwaukee Brewers baseball field, Miller Park. I drove there from the city, which was about a ten-minute drive. It was a fairly nice baseball field, and it had a few statues of the former players as well as some current players and writing on the walls. At the ballpark, I stayed for about an hour, read some of the history, and took some pictures.

The last stop was in Madison. I drove there from Milwaukee (about one and a half hours over eighty miles). Actually, a few years previously, I had been in Madison for two or three days when my cousin Abha and cousin-in-law Prasant got married.

This time around, there was some sort of fair going on during the day, so the city was very crowded, and I had a hard time finding a parking spot. The capitol was up on higher ground, so I could see the building even from a distance. I visited the capitol building and the city a little bit. I also stopped at a Dick's Sporting Goods store to buy some Wisconsin sports memorabilia. That's where I also bought an Aaron Rodgers jersey for AJ.

While I was in Madison, I played golf with four people. On the front nine, I played with two sisters, Ann and Jacque. They were very nice. Ann told me that she was in the hotel property business. When they asked where I was staying, I told them I usually stay at Marriott (unless the town or city doesn't have one). Jacque didn't like that. I found out later that Marriott was the rival of her business. Neither of the sisters belonged to this club; they just came to play one round of golf there. After the round, they signed my golf shirt. I also took their pictures, and we exchanged business cards.

I was actually planning to play golf with another group originally. However, when I approached the two and asked whether I could join them, the father said the son was visiting from out of town and they were trying to have father-son time. I totally understood.

Then, on the back nine, I played with two gentlemen from Korea who had lived in Madison for the last thirty years. Both of them were members at the Bridges Golf Club. They were kind of shy guys. As usual, I took some pictures with them as I do with all golfers I play with. It was a great time!

Golf Course Name:	Bridges Golf Course
Address and Website:	2702 Shopko Dr., Madison, WI 53704 http://www.golfthebridges.com/

Capital Players/ Club Contacts:	Mark, Ann, Jacque
Comment:	*"I received your beautiful family Christmas card today. And I'm still in Wisconsin! But I will return to Florida on Sunday. I will send a copy of your note and one photo to Jacque. That was very sweet of you to send us photos . . . great reminder. It was good to hear that you have completed one of the items on your bucket list. If you get to Naples, Florida, again, please phone and we can 'play a round' at The Club Pelican Bay again. I will keep your invitation in my important social file too."*
Highlight:	Playing golf with a great group of people in Madison was wonderful. Visiting Lambeau Field, taking pictures next to the Vince Lombardi statue, and walking around the stadium in Green Bay was great. I also loved stopping in Milwaukee and walking around the city as well as seeing the Brewers MLB park.

IOWA "HAWKEYE STATE" – 14TH CAPITAL

From Madison, Wisconsin, to Des Moines, Iowa, is about a five-hour drive covering three hundred miles (Routes I-151S and I-80W).

During the trip, I first drove southwest on Route 151, then drove straight west to Route 80. It was not a long drive, but I made a couple of stops. Usually while I am driving, if I see some interesting places or views along the way, I like to stop and check it out. These kinds of short stops were also good for stretching my legs and getting some coffee and snacks.

On my trips, I usually set my destination in my Garmin GPS, but I also use Google Maps or Waze for live traffic directions. Probably about fifty miles before Des Moines, I turned off my Garmin because it kept asking me to go a different route than

I wanted. I arrived in the city in the early evening, and since I was close to the state capitol building and government buildings and mall, I parked and walked around a little bit. I was already in the city, so I started using my Garmin again for directions. However, for some reason, my Garmin didn't want to take me to the hotel. Probably she was mad because I had used Google Maps earlier instead of her. Finally, I was able to make it work and arrived at the hotel.

That day, Des Moines had some kind of festival going on in the city. A lot of music and big crowds made the evening more enjoyable. After I checked in at the Marriott, I walked around the area and had a tasty dinner.

The next morning, I drove around Des Moines and stopped at a few places. It was a fairly small city but pretty. I wanted to visit the state capitol in the morning again. There was a 5K race event happening later, so most of the roads near the capitol building were blocked, but I was able to find a detour route to get to my destination. The capitol building looked much better in the morning, especially in the sunlight. While I was there, I spoke to two groups. They had family and friends running in the 5K. I also asked a young father from the second group about two golf courses where I had tee times. He recommended Waveland Golf Course.

At one point when I was driving, I was on a little higher ground, and when I gazed out at the city in the sunshine, it looked very colorful! At the stoplight, I took a picture.

From there, I started driving to the golf course. I thought I had arrived, but the Garmin took me to the wrong place because they were working on one side of the course on a few holes (as I found out later, this work had been going on for about a year). Unfortunately, the Garmin couldn't detect that.

So I used Google Maps for the latest route, and it was just five to seven minutes away from where I had ended up. I checked in at the pro shop and met three gentlemen with whom I would be playing shortly. Then, I called the other golf course (my backup) and canceled the tee time there.

Waveland Golf Course had some hilly and wooded areas. I also found out that this course had had an amateur golf event recently. When a golf course holds big tournaments, that typically means it is a very good golf course because it has to be maintained quite well for those types of events.

Scott, Brian, and Dan were family members. The father came with his son to see his daughter and son-in-law from South Dakota. They all played well, especially the father, Scott. He had one bad hole, but I also had a couple of bad holes. That's how it goes in golf. Luckily, I played fairly well overall. There were a few holes on the course that looked particularly pretty, so I took some pictures, and I also took a few group pictures with those I played with.

After the round, we all sat down in the clubhouse and had drinks. At that point, we talked and exchanged phone numbers. I also asked them to sign my golf T-shirt, which I was carrying with me. While I was there, I sent one of our group pictures to Brian. Afterward, he sent those pictures to Scott and Dan.

I also texted and sent a few pictures to Shyam, my brother-in-law, and Shashi, my cousin. Shyam and the family had lived in Iowa for a couple of years, so we exchanged a few texts. It was great to feel connected to them as I wrapped up my time in Iowa.

Golf Course Name:	Waveland Golf Course
Address and Website:	4908 University Ave., Des Moines, IA 50311 https://golfwaveland.com/

Capital Players/ Club Contacts:	Scott S., Brian S., and Dan D.
Comment:	*"Well done!"*
Highlight:	Iowa's state capitol was probably one of the best. I even went there twice. Outside of Des Moines, there were miles and miles of cornfields. The farmland looked very cool! Because Shyam, Shashi, and Shaswot had lived in Des Moines, it felt like I had already been to Iowa.

ILLINOIS "LAND OF LINCOLN STATE" – 15TH CAPITAL

From Des Moines, Iowa, to Springfield, Illinois, is about five hours and a 335-mile drive (Routes I-80E and I-74 E).

Driving from Des Moines to Springfield was not so bad. I drove mostly on Routes 80, 74, 155, and 55. I was driving to my last state of this golf trip.

Sometimes, I like to listen to some music, but most of the time, I prefer to focus on driving, especially since these are all new roads/areas for me. Driving for hours and hours, playing golf, visiting cities, seeing important places, and then moving on to the next capital/state over the course of several days sometimes made me tired. Of course, this level of activity would probably make anybody tired! So I wanted to make sure I was driving safely and concentrating on the road.

When I was driving on Route 155, all of a sudden, in the middle of the highway, I saw a huge overpass. It was new and colorful, so it caught my attention right away. Then, I started thinking, *Why is this big overpass in the middle of the highway? I don't see any shopping malls or big cities on either side.* I thought this was strange. But as soon as I passed, I realized it was not an overpass—it was a tollbooth. I had run through without paying! "Oh, man!" I groused to myself. "This is a rental car. What a hassle."

For another couple of hours, I drove on Route 155 until I found another tollbooth and there was someone there. I stopped and explained to the person that I'd driven through without paying and didn't know whether I could pay at this tollbooth now. The staff said I couldn't pay there, but he gave me a paper with directions on how I could pay online. After thanking the man, I took the paper and left. Then, after driving for another thirty minutes or so, I abruptly remembered that earlier that year I had passed a similar overpass near Kearney, Nebraska, without paying the toll. The rental company later charged me.

Although I knew that the state of Illinois was pretty, it still surprised me how beautiful it was. Attractive farms and bright red silos beside the highway were entertaining to look at along the way. I had kind of expected these types of pretty farms and scenery alongside the highway in Wisconsin and Iowa, but Illinois was much prettier.

In Springfield, the hotel was very close to a few dining establishments and the strip mall. It was very easy to walk to the restaurants for dinner and lunch and to the store to buy souvenir items. This was also the first time I saw Marriott hotels with a few parking spots saying, "Reserved for Marriott Rewards Cardholder." Of course, I parked my car there.

In Springfield, I drove around the city and stopped at a couple of places. I also went to the capitol building. But once I got there, I realized that I had forgotten to bring my small travel bag, which had some other things that I needed. So I drove back to the hotel and returned to the capitol building shortly thereafter. I spent about an hour walking around. It was a small area with a reflecting pool similar to our National Mall in Washington, D.C.

I had made a tee time at Lincoln Greens Golf Course in Springfield. I drove there and checked in at the pro shop. Then, I played with Dave and Bill, a father and son. Both of them were decent golfers, but Bill played more consistently. As always, I took some pictures of the golf course and also took a couple of pictures with Dave and Bill. The course was public but still pretty good. I liked the wooded areas. I also invited Bill and Dave to play in D.C. if they ever visit. Bill was very happy to receive the invitation and said he would love to play one round of golf in the nation's capital. I bought a T-shirt, a hat, and a few other things at the pro shop before leaving.

Lincoln, Nebraska, and Springfield, Illinois, airports are fairly similar and small. It seemed like passengers would come only an hour before their flights. Since I was two hours early at both of these airports, I only saw a handful of people except in the stores and car rental places. Even the individuals working at the counter came only an hour before the flights.

While I was in Springfield, Dave had given me a small stone with some writing on it. Since I travel around the country, he asked me to drop off that stone at any other airport in the U.S.

This reminded me of around 2004 or 2005 when my daughter, Monica, asked me to send this Flat Stanley (a book character) cardboard piece to her cousin Jason in Kathmandu, which I did. Jason took Flat Stanley to different places and wrote about himself. Then, Jason mailed Flat Stanley back to Monica. I guess around that time, it was like a Flat Stanley fever going around the world.

It seemed to me that something similar was going on with this stone. People would take it from one airport or location to another, leaving it in a new place. Then, someone else would bring that stone to a different city or country and write about it. There was a specific number written on the stone, and when they entered that number on social media, it was connected to the sender and his group. When I told Dave that I dropped off the stone at the Washington Dulles (IAD) airport, he was very happy.

Golf Course Name:	Lincoln Greens Golf Course
Address and Website:	700 E Lake Shore Drive, Springfield, IL 62712 http://springfieldparks.org/
Capital Players/ Club Contacts:	Bill K. (father) and Dave
Comment:	*"Very cool that you got them all!"*
Highlight:	Seeing Abraham Lincoln's statue in front of the capitol dome and being in the state of Illinois, it felt like I was indeed at the home of Lincoln.

9/24/2017

Annapolis, Maryland

Maryland "Chesapeake State" – 16th Capital

From South Riding, Virginia, to Annapolis, Maryland, is about an hour and fifteen minutes and a seventy-mile drive (Route 50E).

Annapolis is the capital of Maryland. It has only one golf course: the United States Naval Academy Golf Club. To play at this course, you have to either be in the military, or you have to go with a retired/active military service member. My Friday Night Golf League team member Lonnell has a military background, so the two of us went there to play one round of golf. Since we arrived early, we went to the state capitol building first and walked around a little bit.

Then, we went to the golf course. They had a very big pro shop with a great selection of golf apparel. Since we still had about forty-five minutes before our tee time, we bought some golf shirts, hats, and a few other things.

The course was decent. At the first tee box, I met another guy from my company who worked in the Annapolis area but was playing with his own group. Usually, four people play in one group, but we didn't have another twosome to play with, so Lonnell and I ended up playing by ourselves. I played okay, but I still shot over my handicap. Nonetheless, I enjoyed playing at the United States Naval Academy Golf Club with Lonnell.

After the game, we stopped in downtown Annapolis. Lonnell and I bought a few things at different stores there. We also went to a restaurant at the harbor and had dinner before driving back home.

(Whenever my family and friends are visiting us from other states or from Nepal, I usually take them to Washington, D.C., Annapolis, and Baltimore. So I have probably been to Annapolis more than twenty times. I like downtown Annapolis and the harbor.)

Golf Course Name:	US Naval Academy Golf Club
Address and Website:	44 Greenbury Point Rd., Annapolis, MD 21402 https://usnagolf.com/
Capital Players/ Club Contacts:	Lonnell F.
Comment:	*"Now you finished the sixteenth capital. Congratulations!"*
Highlight:	Playing at the military base course with Lonnell was special.

10/28/2017

Trenton, New Jersey

New Jersey "Garden State" – 17th Capital

From South Riding, Virginia, to Trenton, New Jersey, is about a four-hour drive covering two hundred miles (Route I-95 N).

The city of Trenton has only one golf course, and it is private. If a golf course is private, the public can't just go and play, but members can bring their friends with them to play. Members usually like to play on the weekends, so it is hard to book a tee time at private courses for non-members during these times.

I requested that our club's GM (who oversaw five other sister courses within a one-hundred-mile radius of Virginia) to talk to Trenton Country Club. He had contacted the club and talked to Brian, explaining the reason why I wanted to play there in Trenton. Luckily, Brian agreed and asked our GM to send me out to play on Saturday around 11:00 a.m. I left home around six in the morning and arrived at the course at 10:00 a.m.

I went to the pro shop and introduced myself to Brian, then tried to pay by credit card. For some reason, my credit card was not working, so I had to pay with cash. This is the exact reason I like to carry some cash—just in case. I was happy that I had cash on hand! Our club's GM had worked out a special deal for me to play there, so I only had to pay one hundred dollars for the green fee.

Brian went outside and talked to the starter (the golf club employee who lets people tee off on their tee times), who asked me to join a threesome, Chung, Virgil, and Buddy. It was October, but in the middle of the day, the temperature hit seventy degrees. It was truly a perfect day to play golf. Chung, Virgil, and Buddy were great people to play with. Chung was the member, so he had invited his friends to play, and I was pleased to join them. All three were from the Philadelphia area, but Chung said after graduating from Princeton, he had stayed in Trenton and had been working in the area.

Although I like to improve every time I play in different capitals, I am not in the capital for the sole reason of competing and shooting better than my opponents. Although improving is good, enjoying the company of the new people I meet is more important for me. We took a couple of group selfies, and I also asked Chung to take some pictures of me on the course.

After the round, we sat at the clubhouse restaurant and had some snacks and drinks. I left the restaurant thanking them for letting me join their group, and I also invited them to play golf at my club when they come to D.C.

Then, I went back to the pro shop and bought a couple of golf shirts, a hat, and a few other things. I thanked Brian for inviting me and letting me play at his course.

On the drive back to Virginia, I had a quick dinner at one of the stops in Delaware. Driving back took a little more than four hours, but it was not that bad. I have driven the New Jersey Turnpike so many times when picking up my parents from JFK airport when they came from Nepal and taking family to New York City for tours. Over the years, I've experienced bad traffic on the New Jersey Turnpike (two lanes then), but now, most parts have more than two lanes. More importantly, the new service areas for food and the gas stations are much better now.

The next day, I sent email to our club GM letting him know that it was a pleasure meeting Brian and I'd enjoyed playing there. I also thanked him for arranging for me to play at

Trenton Country Club. Additionally, I sent an email to Brian, thanking him for letting me play at his course. He replied, "It was a pleasure meeting with you," and he wished me safe travels with my journey for the remaining courses.

Golf Course Name:	Trenton Country Club
Address and Website:	201 Sullivan Way, Trenton, NJ 08628 https://www.trentoncc.com/
Capital Players/ Club Contacts:	Chung, Virgil, and Buddy
Comment:	*"Happy to hear that you are traveling to play golf in different capitals."*
Highlight:	I enjoyed playing with a great group of people. I was surprised to see part of the New Jersey Turnpike and how nicely they had expanded the roads. There are better service areas now.

2/24/2018

Raleigh, North Carolina

North Carolina "Tar Heel State" – 18th Capital

From South Riding, Virginia, to Raleigh, North Carolina, is about a five-hour drive covering 280 miles (Route I-95 S).

One Friday, I had a work meeting in Chester, Virginia (south of Richmond). Since Raleigh is only two and a half hours from Chester, I was planning to drive down there after to play one round of golf. Our meeting started at 10:00 a.m. and finished around 3:00 p.m. At that time, I drove down to Raleigh.

I had driven on that part of the highway a few times before, so it was not much fun driving again. Once I arrived in North Carolina, I stopped first in the city. Part of Raleigh looked kind of older, but another part looked pretty modern. I went around the capitol building, which didn't have a dome and seemed like the smallest building of all the capitals I had visited at that point. Their government building is also fairly small; it's a two-story building on the opposite side from the capitol.

I also stopped at a souvenir shop to buy a North Carolina Tar Heels basketball T-shirt and hat for AJ. Then, I drove to Marriott, which was on the other side of Raleigh but just a ten-minute drive. When I checked in at the hotel, they gave me a small bag with a few things in it since I am a gold member.

While I was getting in the room, my sister Sharada Didi called, and we spoke a little bit. My sister and nephew were leaving for Nepal in a few days. Then, I texted Nora to let her know that I'd arrived and checked in at the hotel in Raleigh. It was Friday, so I also called Buwa-Muwa (my parents) in Nepal. I call them every Friday evening (Saturday morning in Nepal).

The next morning, I had breakfast at the hotel and then went back to the capitol building area. It looked much prettier in the morning sun. The city looked much better too.

Then, I put the golf course's address in the GPS and drove there. However, once I got to that address, I couldn't find the golf course. Google Maps told me the course was right there, but it was nowhere to be found. So I called the golf course staff and found out that the course was somewhere else. It seemed there was some sort of mix-up. Finally, I decided to call my backup course to tell them that I was coming.

I checked in at the pro shop and bought some souvenirs because I had almost forty-five minutes before my tee time. I joined Andrew and Steve (local guys) and played a round of golf with them. They worked in the IT field. Steve said he was coming to the D.C. area next month for training. I told him if he gave me a call when he was in town, we could play a round of golf. We then exchanged phone numbers. I also texted him a couple of the group pictures we had taken earlier.

The River Ridge Golf Club was fairly good. Some holes were on higher ground, starting with hole one. The greens were very fast. I had a decent round.

It was an unusually warm day for the month of February and a nice day to play golf. I finished my round at 3:30 p.m. and had a late lunch at the clubhouse. I enjoyed my day!

Golf Course Name:	River Ridge Golf Club
Address and Website:	3224 Auburn Knightdale Rd., Raleigh, NC 27610 http://www.golfriverridge.com/
Capital Players/ Club Contacts:	Andrew and Steve
Comment:	*"That's great and good luck!"*

Highlight:	A few holes were especially great-looking. The city of Raleigh looked pretty in the morning but even prettier at night.

4/1/2018

DOVER, DELAWARE

DELAWARE "THE FIRST STATE" – 19TH CAPITAL

From South Riding, Virginia, to Dover, Delaware, is two hours and thirty minutes and a 130-mile drive (Route 50 E).

It was Good Friday before Easter Sunday. Nora and I went to church on Friday evening for the Good Friday service. Then, on Sunday, we attended 6:30 a.m. Easter service. I like Easter morning service because most is done outside. It is kind of chilly around this time of the month and early in the morning, which feels better to me, and it always reminds me of Nepal.

Since Nora had to teach at the church later that morning and I was planning to play one round of golf in Dover, Delaware, we came to church in two cars. After the service, the church served breakfast. Once we were done eating, I left to go to Dover, Delaware, and Nora stayed at the church to teach.

In the 1990s, Nora's parents used to rent a beachfront house for two weeks at Bethany Beach every year for family reunions so everyone from Oregon, New York, Maryland, and Washington, D.C., could come and see each other. As a result, I have driven on this road many times before and am very familiar. To go to Dover, I would go straight 301 North after the Bay Bridge and then go to 50 East going toward Bethany Beach/Ocean City.

Part of Delaware is still poor. It reminded me of some southern states. I could see small rambler houses alongside the highway. Most of these were not well-maintained, but when we reached the small towns, they were somewhat better.

First, I stopped at Dover, the capital of Delaware. Because of what I had seen along the highway (run-down housing and neighborhoods), when I caught sight of Dover, I was actually surprised. The government buildings had probably been built in the mid-1960s and were attractive and well-maintained. The mall, walking area, and streets were fairly enjoyable, and I had a good time strolling around there.

Then, I drove to the golf course. When I arrived, I realized the course was inside the military basecamp, so I was not allowed in. When I had booked the tee time a few days previously, they hadn't said anything about the basecamp. Otherwise, I would have called another golf course instead. But as you know, I always have a backup golf course just in case.

I called the second golf course, and they had the tee time available, so I drove there. The pro shop staff mentioned that after a few hours, they would need to close the pro shop. But obviously the course and other staff would still have someone to take care of the carts, and the restaurant would still be open. Since the pro shop would be closed when I finished my golf round, I bought a few golf course souvenirs, a light long sleeve shirt, a hat, and a couple of other things.

I played with David and Chris (father and son) at the Maple Dale Country Club. They were very kind and engaging people. I had a great conversation with them, and they were very happy to hear why I had come to play one round of golf in Dover at their course.

I played decent, but I only had one birdie. The course was a bit wet that day. I had three bad shots, including one ball I hit in the water on a par three hole. Getting up at five in the morning, driving, and kind of rushing to play makes it a little challenging sometimes—but still, there are no excuses! The golf course was fairly decent but not the typical country club that I normally see. For the most part, the course was nice and pretty.

After the round, we exchanged phone numbers, and I texted David a couple of our group pictures, which I had taken earlier with them. Plus, I invited them to visit Washington, D.C., and join me for a round of golf there. David said he would love to play one round of golf in the nation's capital. Then, I stopped for some sandwiches before heading home.

A few miles before the Bay Bridge, traffic started getting heavier because it was Sunday evening. However, the vehicles were still moving, and I arrived home before it was dark out. I don't like to drive at night, so most of the time, I prefer to get to my destination before the sun sets. This is just to avoid driving at night.

Golf Course Name:	Maple Dale Country Club
Address and Website:	180 Maple Dale Circle, Dover, DE 19904 http://mapledalecc.com/
Capital Players/ Club Contacts:	David and Chris (Father and Son)
Comment:	*"You will finish playing in all the capitals . . . that will be awesome."*
Highlight:	Surprisingly attractive capitol building and campus! Extremely polite father and son at the golf course.

4/20/2018–4/22/2018

Nashville, Tennessee
Frankfort, Kentucky
Charleston, West Virginia

Tennessee "Volunteer State" – 20th Capital

From South Riding, Virginia, to Nashville, Tennessee, is about a ten-hour drive covering 650 miles (Routes I-81S and I-40W).

One week, I had some other appointments that were canceled at the last minute, so I needed to make a quick plan for my trip. It was Friday, and I left at 5:30 in the morning to go to Nashville, Tennessee, from Virginia. Since I had packed the night before, it was not so bad waking up at 5:00, getting ready, and leaving home by 5:30. I always enjoy driving early in the morning. Sometimes, it reminds me of when I was a teenager taking the bus to go to Birgunj, Dharan, and Dhangadhi in Nepal.

I drove from 66 West less than seventy-five miles, then from 81 South, which was over three hundred miles on one road. Usually, I like to take pictures of the welcome signs for each state, driving slowly in the right lane without stopping. Or sometimes I stop near the welcome center. When I was about to enter the state, I saw a "Welcome to Tennessee" sign. I was slowing down and about to take a picture with one hand when, all of a sudden, I spotted a police car on the left side. He was just about to come behind me. Luckily, the visitor center was less than a few hundred yards away. So as soon as I saw that police car, I quickly dropped the phone on the car floor and took the right turn at the visitor center. That was a close one—I almost lost my clean driving record!

I usually pay attention to traffic signs, billboards, etc., as I travel. I liked one creative flashing sign on the highway on this trip: "If you are texting, you are not driving." But I also saw a "Hungry Mother State Park" exit sign. Last but not least, this drive was the first time I saw a car with a Nova Scotia license plate on the road in the U.S.

Part of the highway from Knoxville to Nashville looked pretty with green mountains and scenery similar to Route 66 going west from Gainesville to Front Royal. I drove directly to Harpeth Hills Golf Course in Nashville. I had my tee time at 4:00 p.m., and I arrived there around 3:00. I texted Nora and AJ to let them know I had gotten to the golf course in Nashville a little early. Nora replied, "It's Hajur, and of course you got there early." Just a few hours before I arrived, I realized I would be in the Midwest time zone, one hour behind. I had completely forgotten about the extra hour for me.

I checked in at the pro shop, then found two local guys, Andrew and Andy, who were about to start. I spoke to the starter, and he recommended that I join them, so I did. Andrew and Andy were young, nice, fun guys to play with. I told them why I was in town, and they recommended some places to visit in Nashville.

Usually, I buy a golf shirt and hat after my round, but they had told me earlier that they would close the pro shop around 6:30 p.m. So after nine holes, I stopped quickly at the pro shop and bought a long sleeve golf shirt, a hat, and a few other things. Then, I rejoined Andrew and Andy on hole eleven and finished playing the back nine with them. Some holes in the course were exceptionally pretty!

We took our selfie pictures and exchanged phone numbers, and I texted a couple of photos to both of them. Andrew told me that he comes to the D.C. area every once in a while, and he would contact me when he came next time so we could play golf together.

After golfing, I checked in at the Marriott Residence Inn. Since it was getting late, I didn't want to go out to eat. Instead, I ordered takeout.

The next morning, I had breakfast at the hotel. Then, I went to downtown Nashville. It is a very pretty city with lots of character. First, I parked at the capitol building area and walked around. Just across from the capitol, there are museums and theaters in the heart of downtown. I visited these places. Then, I drove to the other side of the city, parked my car in a garage, and strolled around. I also went to the Riverside area and walked there.

My last stop was at the Titans NFL stadium, which was on the other side of the river. The stadium looked very impressive by the water. I drove there and took a few pictures of Nashville from the stadium side. The city of Nashville looked very colorful and beautiful from the other side of the river in the sunshine.

On the way back from Tennessee, I started thinking that I drove 649 miles/1,051 kilometers and played eighteen holes of golf in the same day. Then, I started thinking about Nepal. I believe the distance from Mechi to Mahakali (east to west) is about one thousand kilometers. So I drove further than Mechi to Mahakali in one day and also played golf. Sounds crazy!

Nora visited Nashville five or six years earlier on a business trip. She said Nashville is beautiful, and after visiting myself, I must say I concur!

Golf Course Name:	Harpeth Hills Golf Course
Address and Website:	2424 Old Hickory Blvd., Nashville, TN 37221 https://www.nashville.gov/Parks-and-Recreation/Golf-Courses/Harpeth-Hills-Golf-Course.aspx/
Capital Players/ Club Contacts:	Andrew T. and Andy S.
Comment:	*"Thanks and congrats on meeting your goal! Glad to hear that you made it through."* *"I agree, a very big accomplishment. I am honored to have been part of it."*
Highlight:	Nashville is a beautiful city by the river. Crossing the bridge to go to the other side in the tourist area offered a stunning view. There were incredible bands and music in the evening and in the morning. The Tennessee Titans NFL stadium looked very pretty. When I was at the stadium and looked back at city . . . it looked so colorful and beautiful!

KENTUCKY "BLUEGRASS STATE" – 21ST CAPITAL

From Nashville, Tennessee, to Frankfort, Kentucky, is about three and a half hours and a 220-mile drive (Routes I-65 N and KY-9002 E).

I drove from Nashville, Tennessee, to Frankfort, Kentucky, going northeast. Some parts of Kentucky have beautiful mountains, which are captivating. There were cattle grazing in the fields, and I also saw freight trains smoothly moving alongside the small mountains. Just gorgeous!

I was heading to Kentucky to play a round of golf at Frankfort Country Club. I had called them before I left Washington, but the club had asked me whether someone from my club could give them a call first. If we are planning to play golf at a private country club, usually our own club has to contact the other one, and there is a form they need to fill out. So I had sent an email to our club GM with the contact info of Frankfort Country Club, and he had spoken to the golf pro there. Ultimately, my tee time was set for around 2:30 p.m., and I received email confirmation from our GM. It was very generous of him to contact the course.

I played one round of golf at Frankfort Country Club. The golf course had a big clubhouse and a lovely restaurant facing the eighteenth hole. I went to the clubhouse, but the golf pro was not there. However, he had told his staff that I was coming, so they were expecting me.

At the clubhouse, I introduced myself and asked whether I could join another player. The staff told me someone had just left. One of the staff members went to grab that player but came back saying he couldn't find them. Perhaps the player had already finished two or three holes. So I went to the first tee box alone.

However, by the middle of the first fairway, I found that single player coming back on the ninth hole from the other side. I reached out to him and asked whether I could join him. He said, "No problem. Let's start on the back nine." His name was Kevin, and he was not a member, but his father, who lived inside the gated community, was. He showed me his dad's house, a beautiful home close to one of the holes. Most houses looked very pretty alongside the golf course.

The course was inside a gated community, but the way it was designed, I never felt like I was playing golf inside of it. The Frankfort Country Club was a beautiful golf course; the fairways were like carpet, and the greens were excellent. I had never played on a course this well-maintained. It was the middle of April, and most courses are still dry and brown that time of year, but the fairways and greens of this course were absolutely stunning!

I took a couple of pictures with Kevin and texted those to him. Kevin had to leave after the sixteenth hole, but I reconnected with him at the parking lot so he could sign my golf travel shirt before he left. Then, I went back to play another nine holes on the front nine where I met another gentleman, Al.

Al was a military veteran who had completed thirty years of service and recently retired. When I said that I had come from Nashville, he said he'd lived in Nashville for a few years and knew most of the courses in the area. As we finished playing the front nine, I took a picture with Al and texted him. After that, I went back to holes seventeen and eighteen to complete my full eighteen holes. After the round, I returned to the pro shop, paid my green fee, and bought a sweater, a hat, and a logo ball.

I really enjoyed playing at this beautiful course with Kevin and Al. Hopefully, I will play with them sometime here in Virginia at my club.

From the golf course, I drove to the capitol building. It was a very beautiful capitol with a dome in a quiet area. I walked around the building and around the city a little bit. There was a beautiful garden with lovely decorations around the capitol.

Then, I drove to the hotel, which was about fifteen minutes away. Once I arrived at the Marriott, even before checking in, I asked about restaurants nearby. The staff recommended a couple of options in the center of downtown. Since it was getting dark, I didn't check in but instead went straight to my top choice for dinner, which was about fifteen minutes away. I parked in front of the recommended restaurant, but before going in to eat, I walked around exploring some historic places. The area was fairly small but nice and peaceful.

After strolling around, I came back to the restaurant where I told the waitress that I was not that hungry and asked whether they had some hot soup. In turn, the waitress suggested a special shrimp entrée. So instead of just ordering soup, I also ordered that shrimp entrée, which was actually delicious, and I finished it all. It was a really scrumptious dinner, and I am glad the waitress suggested their special entrée to me.

After leaving that part of Frankfort with restaurants and historic places, which looked very pretty, I returned to the hotel. The next morning, I had breakfast and then left Frankfort, Kentucky, with a great impression of the Frankfort Country Club and the entire capital.

Golf Course Name:	Frankfort Country Club
Address and Website:	101 Duntreath St., Frankfort, KY 40601 https://www.frankfortcountryclub.com/Home/The-Club
Capital Players/ Club Contacts:	Kevin J. and Al N.
Comment:	*"That's great you're playing in the capitals."*
Highlight:	The fairway of this country club was the best one I have seen so far at any golf course. They were all green and well-maintained, almost like carpet. The part of Frankfort with restaurants and historic places looked very pretty!

West Virginia "Mountain State" – 22nd Capital

From Frankfort, Kentucky, to Charleston, West Virginia, is about a three-hour drive covering two hundred miles (Route I-64 E).

The view driving from Frankfort, Kentucky, to Charleston, West Virginia, was really scenic! On part of the drive, I saw some grand houses, but I also spotted some smaller ones that were not well-maintained. I arrived at Charleston around eleven in the morning and drove straight to the capitol area where I parked my car.

Driving down the highway on my way to the capital, I saw Charleston in the valley and spotted a few factories, which weren't too bad looking. The capitol building was alongside the Kanawha River, which runs through the middle of downtown. From one side, I saw the city, and on the other side, striking houses were located above the river on the mountains—just beautiful! Kanawha River is fairly big and powerful. Alongside it, there was a very beautiful walking trail. I enjoyed this incredible view.

While I was traipsing around the capitol building, I met a husband and wife who were from Richmond, Virginia. The husband was playing with a drone using a remote control by the river, and his wife was walking around the capitol. I told them I was from Virginia too, and she was happy to hear that.

This capitol building was one of my favorites—big and beautiful! The campus was definitely the largest that I had seen so far. The other government buildings close by made the place extra majestic! They were vast, complex, and well-maintained. I imagine that those buildings were constructed in the 1930s and 1940s, but they didn't seem that old and were obviously well taken care of. I also walked around one part of the city a little bit. The area was surrounded by mountains, and the river lent a certain charm to the city. Overall, Charleston looked gorgeous!

After seeing the capitol building and getting a quick tour of the city, I stopped for lunch and then drove to the golf course at Berry Hills Country Club. This course was all the way at the top of the hill. I had tried calling this golf course a week before, but nobody had answered the phone. Since this was a country club, another member needed to bring me to this course to play golf. I had called my own golf club and asked our GM whether he could give them a call. He had tried, but they hadn't picked up the phone for him either. It seemed that the reception was not that clear in the mountains. So I decided to drive to this course and talk to one of the members so they could invite me to the course as a guest.

That day, I parked my car and changed into my golf shirt and shoes. Then, I found one gentleman in the parking lot. I asked him whether he belonged to this course, and he said yes. We introduced ourselves to each other, and he told me his name was Tom. I explained that I was from Virginia and had come to play one round of golf at his course. He brought me into the pro shop and introduced me as his friend.

I paid my green fee and went to see Tom and the starter outside. Tom was practicing for a tournament the next day, so he couldn't play with me. Luckily, when I went to the first tee box, I found three players ready to tee off. I asked them whether I could join them, and they agreed.

I played with three gentlemen: Ganpat, Danny, and Jashvant. They were all working in the health field. Danny was a tech guy, and Ganpat and Jashvant were cardiologists. I was happy that I was able to join them. They were wonderful to play with, and I enjoyed talking to them.

The golf course looked pretty, but I knew that between May and June, this course would be even more spectacular. Being up in the mountains and seeing all of the greenery would be fantastic. While we were playing, I took a few pictures with my fellow golfers to commemorate the occasion.

Around hole twelve, I realized I had lost my 4 hybrid club somewhere on a previous hole. I was playing at a golf tournament the next weekend, and that 4 hybrid was my rescue club. I would have a hard time competing without it. When I use it, I can hit 140- to 180-yard shots, so I rely on it much more than any other club in my bag. As you can imagine, I was a little upset that I had lost it. I asked Ganpat to call the clubhouse to see whether anyone had returned it. Of course, he called, but no one answered. However, he assured me that someone would bring it back.

After the round, I bought a golf shirt, a hat, and a logo ball at the pro shop. Everyone signed my golf shirt that I take with me to every state. I also sat down with Danny at the clubhouse restaurant and had a little snack and drink. The pro shop and Ganpat said they would mail my club once they found it, which was very nice of them.

Before I left the course, I went to the car and changed into some comfortable driving clothes and shoes. When I was about to leave, the starter came in the golf cart and said someone had returned my club and that they had been trying to find me. I thanked him and said I appreciated it. What a relief!

Usually, on all my golf trips, people are helpful. But at the Berry Hills Country Club, the members and staff were extremely helpful and friendly. They truly went above and beyond. It felt like I was already a member there. As a result, I left Berry Hills Country Club and Charleston on a high and positive note.

I left the city around 5:00 p.m., and my estimated arrival time home was about 10:00 p.m. I don't like driving at night, but I knew it would still be daylight until about 8:00 p.m. So I would have to drive for about two hours in the dark.

While I was heading home, Waze recommended I go on another route that was about twenty miles shorter. I decided to take it, but as soon as I drove about eight to ten miles, I knew I shouldn't have gone that way. It was dark and hilly, and there were winding roads. I had to drive extremely slowly and carefully, especially because I didn't feel comfortable. Now Waze showed my new estimated time of arrival to be 11:30 p.m. It was getting worse. After some time, there were finally no more hilly and winding roads, but it was still dark. I drove about 125 miles on those treacherous roads in the dark through the West Virginia mountains.

Now I was driving at forty-five miles per hour in a fifty-five-mile-per-hour zone, and it was a one-lane road. There were three or four cars behind me, and I am sure they didn't like that I was driving under the speed limit. Soon after that one-lane road became two lanes, those cars passed me. I said to myself that I know I am not a confident driver in the dark, but I am still a decent driver. Although it was extremely dark, I could see cars' rearview lights, and I could still see roads clearly but nothing else.

I had about seventy miles left, and I didn't want to drive forty-five miles per hour and get home after midnight, so I started to drive right behind the other cars on the road. I had to keep pace to stay behind them in order to see the road clearly. I didn't even see what speed I was going, but I knew I was going fast. At least I was trailing behind the other cars. This was the first time I had ever driven far above the speed limit and didn't feel like I had a choice.

After driving seventy miles on this road, I got onto a different one that I had driven before. This was the same road I used to take to bring AJ and Serena to summer camps. Overall, I was familiar with the area, and the roads were not as bad. I did fine after that. I stopped in Winchester, Virginia, filled up the car with gas, and got some hot coffee. I arrived home after midnight. It was one adventurous night of driving 125 miles in the dark through the West Virginia mountains on one small, winding road!

I played in a three-club tournament at my golf club the weekend after I came back from the West Virginia trip. I won the tournament, my sixth individual title. Finding that 4 hybrid I had lost was very important and helped me win. I sent a text to Ganpat letting him know about the 4 hybrid and the victory.

Golf Course Name:	Berry Hills Country Club
Address and Website:	1 Berry Hills Road, Charleston, WV 25309 https://www.berryhillscc.com/
Capital Players/ Club Contacts:	Ganpat T., Jashvant, Danny S.
Comment:	*"Congratulations and happy holidays to you and your family."*
Highlight:	This country club was up in the mountains. I played in early spring. If I had played in the middle of the spring through early fall, I imagine that this course would have looked absolutely beautiful with the colorful trees. The members whom I played with and the staff at this club were very polite, helpful, and friendly. Losing my 4 hybrid club and having it returned to me was quite notable! Driving through West Virginia on winding, one-lane roads at night for over 175 miles in the mountains and then almost hitting a deer was kind of scary but memorable overall.

5/24/2018–5/29/2018

SACRAMENTO, CALIFORNIA
CARSON CITY, NEVADA
SALT LAKE CITY, UTAH
DENVER, COLORADO
SANTA FE, NEW MEXICO
PHOENIX, ARIZONA

CALIFORNIA "THE GOLDEN STATE" – 23RD CAPITAL

I had a direct flight from Washington to Sacramento. Sometimes, direct flights make travel much easier and save a lot of time. That's why I opted for this type of flight.

About ten miles before arriving at the Sacramento airport, I started seeing farming similar to that in Nepal—pretty! But there were thousands of water pads on the farm. Initially, I thought the airport was like Biratnagar in Nepal, but obviously it was bigger, like the Springfield or Lincoln airports.

After I got off the plane in California, I went to the rental place and rented my car. Then, I drove to the hotel, which was about seventeen or eighteen miles away. As soon as I parked my car in front of the building, I texted Nora letting her know that I had arrived at the hotel in Sacramento.

After I checked in, I found out that they would close the hotel restaurant within the next forty-five minutes. So I went to the room and dropped off my carry-on bag and washed my face before heading downstairs to the restaurant. I was kind of tired and was not that hungry. Since it was late, they already had closed the restaurant section and only had the bar section with small tables open. I sat in that area, then ordered some wings, ate, and went upstairs to my room.

The next morning, I was planning to drive to the capitol building area. However, I discovered the capitol was less than half a mile away, which was perfect because I usually like to walk rather than drive. One thing about staying at the Marriott downtown is that everything is within the city center, and I can typically walk to the city, parks, etc. So I walked to the capitol, which had a beautiful building and campus.

While I was heading toward my destination, I ran into a capitol staff person, and he gave me some history about the Sacramento capitol as well as provided some other suggestions. The capitol was closed in the morning, so the staff person invited me to come later in the day. After that, I walked around the city. It was sunny, and the city looked very pretty. Then, I walked back to the Marriott.

I had breakfast at the hotel before heading to Cordova Golf Course. We started on the back nine, where I played with Steve, Lee, Ben, and Lee, all Korean players. They were very friendly people.

They had one unique tradition in putting. Let's say I putted better than the other players. Then, I would be safe. But everybody else with a tied putting score would do rock, paper, scissors. Whoever lost would need to pick up all the golf balls from the cup and return them to everyone. When they did this, they would laugh and scream, which was very unique and enjoyable! By the second or third hole, I caught on and joined them for this goofy game. They had also brought some snacks, which they shared with me—very generous!

After our round, we took some pictures and exchanged phone numbers, and I texted our group pictures to them. Then, I went to my car and grabbed my golf shirt for all of them to sign. Before they left, I invited them to play a round of golf if they came to the Washington, D.C., area someday.

After that, I played the front nine with Frank and Phil, father and son. I told them that I had already played the back nine and was just joining them for the front nine. They were happy that I joined them. The golf course had mostly par threes and par fours. After the round, I had a quick lunch at the clubhouse.

From there, I drove from Sacramento, California, to Carson City, Nevada. The drive was about three hours and 130 miles (Route US-50 E).

Driving from Sacramento to Carson City was beautiful. Part of it was kind of green, and part of it was characterized by desert-looking mountains. But the houses looked well-maintained, fairly big and pretty. I thought to myself, *I could live here*. While I was driving, Ben C. (my golf partner) called me to talk about the Wednesday Night League (WNL) week five match. Since I had been out that Wednesday, he'd played and won. He wanted to share the news with me. Great gentleman!

Driving through the green mountains was beautiful. I would say this was definitely one of my favorite experiences with driving in different states. Because the roads were narrow and high up in the mountains, it was very hard for cars to pass by. So about every one-tenth of a mile, there was a small area for cars to pull over so other vehicles could pass. I thought that was a smart design by the highway engineer. I used this area to let other cars pass me several times.

On the way to Carson City, I stopped at Placerville, a historic place for gold mining. In the Gold Rush time period, I believe a lot of people became rich from the precious commodity from this place. The town looked very pretty and clean in between the ridges of mountains alongside the highway.

When I was driving downhill on the other side of the mountains, the valley looked very pretty. But I started to see huge black clouds in the sky, which turned into a thunderstorm with heavy rain in the valley. It was raining on me a little bit when I was driving, but it was not the downpour I could see down in the valley near the Lake Tahoe area.

When I reached the valley, I needed to stop at a gas station to fill up the car. I started seeing white stuff on the road and on the ground everywhere. After I parked, I realized it was hail. I got the gas, parked my car, and went inside the store where I asked the store manager whether it was hail on the ground. After all, it looked all sunny and beautiful outside except in this part of Lake Tahoe, and it was hard to believe there was so much hail everywhere. The manager said it was a heavy hailstorm, the likes of which they hadn't seen in the last thirty or so years. "A historic hailstorm," he remarked. It was unbelievable!

Then, all of a sudden, I started thinking that if I had been in the middle of this hailstorm, my car would have been damaged. That would have been a problem because I was driving a rental car. I bought a few souvenir items inside the store and left to go to Lake Tahoe.

When I finally arrived, I stopped to admire the breathtaking scenery. Even in this kind of hot weather in May, I could see some snow on the top of the mountains, which looked very pretty. Lake Tahoe is huge and surrounded by mountains. Part of Lake Tahoe is in California, and the other part is in Nevada. The view and setting with clean water, boats, and mountains looked absolutely gorgeous. It also reminded me a little bit of Fewa Lake in Nepal. Lake Tahoe looked exactly like what we see in photos or on TV—just stunning.

Golf Course Name:	Cordova Golf Course
Address and Website:	9425 Jackson Road, Sacramento, CA 95826 http://www.cordovagc.com/
Capital Players/ Club Contacts:	Steve A, Lee, Ben and Lee, and Frank and Phil
Comment:	*"Hello, dear friend. I have just returned from a short vacation trip and found your mail today. Thank you for the lovely family Christmas card. Meeting you was our pleasure, and we will remember you as a golf member forever. Thank you for your invitation, and I (we) will ask your big favor to be my (our) sightseeing guide if we ever have a chance to visit the nation's capital city Washington, D.C. You are one persistent and willful golfer. I must agree to praise you and congratulate you for being the U.S. fifty capitals golf trip player. Merry Christmas and happy New Year."*
Highlight:	Seeing those big, beautiful, well-maintained homes in the mountains while driving from Sacramento on the way to Carson City as well as seeing beautiful roads on the top of the mountain was very nice. Seeing Placerville, which is a historic place for gold mining during the Gold Rush era, and seeing Lake Tahoe was absolutely amazing! At the golf course in the middle of the round, Steve, Lee, Ben, and Lee shared their homemade snack with me. It was a little thing, but that was special and memorable as well!

NEVADA "SILVER STATE" – 24TH CAPITAL

From Sacramento, California, to Carson City, Nevada, it is about three hours and a 130-mile drive (Route US-50 E).

I drove from Sacramento, California, to Carson City, Nevada. Coming down from the mountains and looking at state of Nevada granted me a very pretty view! I typically enjoy being on the top of the mountains and looking at the valley below.

The drive was lovely from Sacramento to Carson City. I especially enjoyed passing through Lake Tahoe. I had stopped at Lake Tahoe on the California side.

Since I was in Carson City early and the golf course was on the way, I stopped at the Silver Oak Golf Course in Carson City first. I was planning to play eighteen holes of golf there that afternoon. However, the weather didn't look promising. It started lightly raining, and I began to hear a few thunderstorms. The front nine of the course was up in mountains in a hilly area, so it was kind of dangerous to play when we started to hear thunder and see lightning. The golf course closed the front nine for good reason, but the back nine was open.

The course had a league going on, and nobody else was playing except for the league players. Instead of coming back the next morning to play all eighteen holes, I wanted to play nine holes that afternoon and play another nine the next morning to finish my eighteen. So I spoke to a couple of players from the league, and they didn't seem to mind if I joined them.

The last group of the league with foursomes had already started, so I began behind them. Since I was playing alone, I was waiting for them to finish, and it was taking a long time. Finally, on hole three, I approached those guys and asked whether I could join them. Since they were playing in the league, they said I could go in front of them and play if I would like. But I told them it was important to me to play with somebody who belonged to this course due to my golf journey criteria. They didn't have a problem, so all five of us played together.

However, the weather was still not cooperating. It started to rain, and we played as it sprinkled and eventually turned into a little bit of thunder and lightning. Since we were the last group, a person from the club was right behind us, waiting to grab the flag sticks from each hole. At that point, I felt a little bad about the club's staff, since she was waiting behind us, and I knew the golf course couldn't close since we were still playing. I was coming back the next morning to play anyway, so I could have stopped playing anytime if the league players had stopped playing. But overall, since we were all playing, I didn't have a problem golfing even during bad weather conditions.

The foursome I played the back nine with included Ryan, Mike, Wendy, and Bryan, and they were great and easygoing people. Plus, the course was beautiful! I found out from Ryan that he has a brother who works at the military base in southern Virginia. We took a group selfie on the eighteenth hole, and I texted them our group pictures.

After golf, I went straight to the hotel and checked in. The Marriott was next to the main highway but up on higher ground. There was not great visibility, but I could still see part of the city, the mountains, and the valley below from the hotel. Carson City looked very pretty! It reminded me a little bit of Hile, Dhankuta, in Nepal.

Next to the Marriott, there was a casino. Since I was in the state of Nevada, I wanted to go at least once and play for a little bit. But after the long drive and after playing nine holes of golf, I was getting tired.

From the hotel room, I saw Olive Garden a short distance away, and I decided to go there for dinner instead. So I walked to the restaurant, planning to order and eat quickly and then go back to the hotel. To my dismay, the waiter there kept showing me different brands and tastes of wines. Although I appreciated how attentive he was, I told him that I had had a long drive, was tired, and just wanted to have a quick dinner. He understood, but I still kind of felt bad. After dinner, I walked back to the hotel, too tired to do anything but sleep.

When I woke up the next morning, the weather was pretty much the same as the day before. I found out there was a 24/7 Walmart close by, so I drove there and bought some souvenir items like I do in every state that I travel to. Then, I had a quick breakfast before heading to the golf course again.

I joined Jim and Ryan to play the front nine. For the first hour or so, it started to rain again, but this time, there was no thunder or lightning like the day before. If I didn't have a tight schedule, I wouldn't have played in rain again. However, I had to make the rest of the scheduled trips, and I was already behind, so I wanted to play the front nine as soon as I could and leave Carson City. Fortunately, the weather started to get better with the sun shining at the end. The course looked very pretty, especially the front nine up in the mountains, and the view below looked absolutely gorgeous! I knew if it was sunny in the afternoon, the course and Carson City below would look even better.

After the round, I bought some souvenirs from the clubhouse, took a few pictures, bought a cup of coffee, and left Carson City. Jim and Ryan were great guys, and we talked about Nepal and some other things before I left.

On the way from Carson City to Salt Lake City, I stopped in Reno, Nevada, for breakfast. It was too bad I couldn't even play a few bucks at the casino. Reno had lots of casino hotels, and the city looked very pretty because it lies underneath the mountains.

Also in between Carson City and Reno, I saw some interesting billboards. They were very informative and seemed to have double meanings. The first picture was Nobel Prize winner

Malala Yousafzai, and the second picture was a military officer originally from Mexico. Their pictures were not just in one place but in multiple places alongside the highway. I thought that was very smart.

Golf Course Name:	Silver Oak Golf Course
Address and Website:	1251 Country Club Drive; Carson City, NV 89703 http://www.silveroakgolf.com/
Capital Players/ Club Contacts:	Day 1 – Bryan, Mike and Ryan (father and son), and Wendy Day 2 – Ryan and Jim
Comment:	*"What a great day of golf! Thank you for the experience and congrats on a cool quest."*
Highlight:	Driving through the Nevada Desert, briefly visiting Reno, seeing inspiring double meanings of billboard signs, and playing golf in bad weather.

Utah "Mormon/Friendly State" – 25th Capital

From Carson City, Nevada, to Salt Lake City, Utah, is about an eight-hour drive covering 545 miles (Route I-80 E).

Driving from Carson City to Salt Lake City was an enjoyable experience. Part of the drive took me through the mountains. I love driving in the mountains and seeing the valley below. There were also some interesting and creative road signs. I loved them!

I arrived in Salt Lake City, Utah, in the evening. First, I went straight to the state capitol area. Once I got there, I texted Nora to let her know that I had made it to Salt Lake City. Since it was already after 5:00 p.m., the state capitol was closed, but there was a fairly big wedding going on inside the capitol, and a lot of people were gathered outside the building.

It was on a hilltop, so the dome looked very pretty, especially at night with the light shining. It was a big and beautiful capitol building, and the campus had vibrant gardens all around. The city looked lovely in the valley with night light and illumination—the capitol dome, the campus, and the city down below. I asked a person to take a couple of pictures of me in front of the capitol, and he obliged.

I also drove around the city a little bit that evening. Then, I drove to Marriott, which was in the middle of Salt Lake City, and checked in. Since I was tired of driving, I didn't have the energy to do anything. I called room service at the hotel and ate in the room.

It was a large and magnificent Marriott. When I was parking in front of the hotel with a valet person, I knew I didn't look great, and I had only my carry-on bag and golf bag. Incidentally, Nora visited Salt Lake City twenty-five years previously on a business trip, and she stayed at the same Marriott then. Perhaps she made a better first impression!

The next morning, I walked around the city, then had a very tasty but heavy breakfast at the hotel before heading to the golf course.

I played golf at Bonneville Golf Course with Adam, Joe, and Danny. Joe's daughter and family live in Baltimore, so he visits her every once in a while. I invited Joe to play golf at my course when he comes to the D.C. area next time. I took a few group pictures with Joe, Danny, and Adam and texted those pictures to them.

The course was in the mountains—pretty! I could still see some white snow on the top of the peaks at the end of May. The mountains in the back looked very picturesque. It reminded me of Nepal.

On the way from Salt Lake City to Denver, I saw beautiful big red rock mountains alongside the highways, which is typical for the state of Utah. I had seen those Red Mountains in pictures and in movies many times, and I'd always thought they were very pretty. I wanted to see those red rocks close up, so I stopped at one place to take a closer look. They looked even prettier from a near distance.

I also stopped at a scenic area alongside the highway. There was a beautiful lake with mountains rising in the back, and it was a sunny day, so it looked very pretty. It felt like I'd found this place unexpectedly. All of a sudden, it opened up, and I saw a few beautiful blue lakes on the right side. They were so big, and I couldn't even see the other side. They looked like oceans. I stopped there for a while and looked at the view all around. Of course, I also took a few pictures before heading to the road again. I had always thought it would be pretty to drive in Utah because it is green everywhere, and highways are pretty alongside the mountains. I was right—it was gorgeous!

Golf Course Name:	Bonneville Golf Course
Address and Website:	954 Connor Street, Salt Lake City, UT 84108 https://www.slc-golf.com/
Capital Players/ Club Contacts:	Joe C., Adam, and Danny
Comment:	*"I was in Baltimore two weeks ago for some meetings. I hope to be back in the spring. I would love to play out there. Have a happy holiday season, my friend."*

Highlight:	Even in the summertime, I could see some snow on the top of the mountains. Obviously, it is a mountain state, and a lot of people go skiing most of the year. The capitol dome was one of the biggest and most beautiful I had seen. The campus and flowers around thc building looked very pretty. The view of the city down below from the capitol dome looked very pretty at night. Joe said he has a Mount Everest screensaver, which made me happy. Salt Lake City, Utah, was my twenty-fifth capital, which meant I was halfway to my goal, so I will always remember this state.

Colorado "Rocky Mountain State" – 26th Capital

From Salt Lake City to Denver, I took the main highway. The drive was about eight hours and 520 miles (Route I-80 East and I-25 South).

There was a route that was around 150 miles shorter with a scenic view, but sometimes, those shorter routes take longer because of lower speed limits, small roads, mountain curves, etc. So I took route 80 East from Salt Lake City to Denver. I had to go over half of my drive (250 miles) through Wyoming. Then, right below Cheyenne, Rte. 25 runs north to south from near Cheyenne to Denver.

As soon as I started coming down from Cheyenne to Denver on Rte. 25, I could see the flow of traffic. I am not just talking about heavy traffic close to Denver; almost one hundred miles out, traffic was pretty heavy . . . but still moving. I drove directly to the hotel. Unfortunately, I guess the hotel was full, as I had to park my car two blocks away in Marriott's additional parking facility.

Since it was getting late, I went to eat first. Everything was nearby, so I walked to the area with restaurants. I didn't find the place I was looking for, so I ended up going to Chipotle, where I grabbed a chicken burrito and chips, then came back to the hotel and checked in.

The next morning, I went to downtown Denver. This is a very pretty city, especially because of the picturesque mountains—like those in Nepal but not as big. The elevation of Denver is like Kathmandu's elevation. It is one mile from sea level; that's why they call Denver the Mile High City. The capitol dome is very beautiful with a golden color on the top. This dome was not as big as some other mountain states' domes, but it was still a very pretty looking building. Denver is a beautiful city.

From there, I drove to Overland Park Golf Course where I paid the green fee and checked in. Usually, I don't buy golf course souvenirs until I finish playing, but since I had almost an hour before my tee time, I went ahead and bought a golf shirt, a hat, and a few other golf course logo souvenir items ahead of time.

I played with Craig and Charles—super friendly guys! The course was enjoyable but fairly flat. It reminded me of Chantilly Country Club and International Country Club in Virginia. I wanted to take pictures, so Craig asked the cart girl to take our group photo. I thanked her and gave her some money. It was great to see mountains, greens, and beautiful views from the golf course. I enjoyed it!

After the round, we sat down at the clubhouse and had some snacks and drinks. Meanwhile, I texted those pictures to Craig and Charles. Then, I invited them to play a round of golf at my club when they visited Washington, D.C., before saying goodbye to them. I changed my clothes and left the golf course.

When I was leaving, I started thinking, *I have been driving and visiting these mountain states, and they are certainly special.* Definitely Utah and Colorado were two states I most wanted to visit. I thought to myself, *I will return to these places, but most likely, I will visit with my family in the future.*

Fast forward to the beginning of 2022. Our son found a job outside of Denver and moved there! We have already visited him twice. While we were there, we went on a high mountain hiking tour with a guide. It afforded us an absolutely stunning view of the mountains and lakes. We also went on the city tour, where we learned a lot about Denver and its history. Plus, we went to a Colorado Rockies (MLB) baseball game. It was a bit hot, but we enjoyed the atmosphere and the game. We are big fans of Denver!

Golf Course Name:	Overland Park Golf Course
Address and Website:	1801 S. Huron Street, Denver, CO 80223 https://www.cityofdenvergolf.com/overland_park
Capital Players/ Club Contacts:	Craig J. and Charles
Comment:	*"Got everything. Thank you. You've got a great-looking family. Congratulations on finishing your quest. I'd like to hear about your next project."*
Highlight:	Seeing those beautiful Rocky Mountains.

NEW MEXICO "LAND OF SUNSHINE/CACTUS STATE" – 27TH CAPITAL

From Denver, Colorado, to Santa Fe, New Mexico, is about a six-hour drive covering 390 miles (Route I-25 S).

I drove from Denver, Colorado, to Santa Fe, New Mexico, which is such a colorful state. Even before entering New Mexico, I started seeing vibrant, colorful license plates. Plus, the houses were a little different in style, and some of them were colorful too. Even the cattle were not just black; some were light red. There were open fields, some greenery, and miles and miles of beautiful land I could see driving from the highway. When I saw those houses that were multi-colored, it reminded me of Nepal.

Before entering New Mexico, I spotted a parking area where they had a "Welcome to New Mexico" billboard. People were stopping, so I stopped there too. Of course, the billboard was bright yellow, and in the late afternoon, the sunlight made it appear very pretty and bright. Also, that area was on the high ground, so from there, the view of New Mexico looked beautiful!

I eventually checked in at the Marriott Fairfield Inn. The hotel was only two or three stories but kind of square and long. My room in the hotel was on the second floor and on the opposite side of the lobby. It may have had something to do with me being tired after such a long drive, but it felt like I had to walk one-tenth of a mile from the lobby to my room and vice versa. As an elite platinum member of Marriott, I usually find that the hotel staff and their system do fairly well in terms of accommodating the guests in the best way possible regarding upgrading the room to a quieter one that's closer to the elevator and so on. They gave me an upgraded and quiet room at the Fairfield Inn, but it was not close to the elevator or the lobby.

The next morning, I had breakfast at the hotel and then drove to the state capitol. New Mexico's state capitol is unlike any other. It is not a dome or a regular building; it is a rotunda, which is unique and visually interesting! It was Memorial Day. In the morning, the capitol area was fairly quiet, and not many people were walking. I walked around and took a few pictures. I also asked a few questions to and chatted a bit with a lady who was walking her dog around the capitol area. There were no high-rises, mostly two-story buildings. Parts of New Mexico reminded me a little bit of cities like Biratnagar, Birgunj, and Bhairahawa in Nepal. After visiting the downtown area, I drove around different parts of the city to explore a little bit.

Then, I drove to the golf course. I checked in at Santa Fe Country Club and paid the green fee. They were doing a lot of renovation work at the course. I could see light yellow and red soil all over the place. Rudy and Cliff let me join their group to play. I enjoyed playing with them. I played fairly well, especially considering it was my first time on this course.

We also took a few selfies together. After the round, we asked a club staff member to take our group picture, and she did. I texted those photos to Rudy and Cliff. Before they left, I invited them to visit D.C. Then, I bought a golf shirt, a hat, and a ball marker before leaving the golf course.

I stopped in Gallup City to buy a few New Mexico souvenir items as well. I remember pausing at the final rest stop area in the state where I looked at the view for the last time in New Mexico. It was very pleasant and pretty!

Golf Course Name:	Santa Fe Country Club
Address and Website:	4360 Country Club Road, Santa Fe, NM 87507 https://www.santafecountryclub.com/
Capital Players/ Club Contacts:	Rudy M. and Cliff U.
Comment:	*"Nice meeting you and enjoy your travels."*
Highlight:	New Mexico is such a colorful state; the houses and even the cattle were different colors. The license plates in New Mexico were not just colorful but also shiny. They looked very pretty. Those plates and homes (like Biratnagar) will always remind me of Santa Fe and New Mexico. A great state!

Arizona "Grand Canyon State" – 28th Capital

I drove from Santa Fe, New Mexico, to Phoenix, Arizona, which is about an eight-hour and 480-mile drive (Route I-40 W).

Once I entered Arizona, I stopped at a rest stop and texted Nora, "Now I am 307 miles to Phoenix." At the rest stop, I took a picture of the Arizona state billboard. It was a colorful billboard in the desert! I had started seeing billboard advertisements of the Navajo Nation, the world's largest reservation, all the way from New Mexico. There was billboard after billboard of Navajo Nation alongside the highway in many places.

Now that I was in Arizona, I could see the typical Arizona desert scene along with red mountains and cliffs. I could view dry desert land for miles and miles. It was so striking and pretty!

About one hundred miles before Phoenix, the drive through the mountains became absolutely stunning. It was the month of May, and the trees and forest looked all green and vibrant! It reminded me a little bit of Tribhuvan Highway in Nepal in terms of winding roads, but the driving was more like in the West Virginia mountains, all verdant and beautiful. It was getting late, so part of the drive was in daylight and part was at nighttime. Especially at night, it looked very pretty! I could see the bright moon on one side, and I could see eight to ten miles of lines of cars on the other side of the mountains.

Although people were driving, everything seemed very peaceful. Perhaps the big ridges of the mountains were absorbing the noises. This quietness kind of reminded me of the quietness of Antarctica. Then, I laughed to myself, *How am I comparing Antarctica and Arizona right now?* Comparing the desert I had seen a few hours ago and all the green mountains I was seeing now was different but kind of neat!

I parked my car in front of the hotel in the valet parking area and went inside the lobby to check in. The hotel room service and restaurant were about to close, so before I went to my room, I ordered takeout dinner. I was on the seventeenth floor, and the skyline from the hotel room looked very pretty. The NBA arena and MLB field were two blocks away from the hotel. There were no buildings between, so the view was very clear from the hotel. At the counter, the staff had told me this hotel was brand new, so the building looked very new and fancy.

The weather was supposed to be hot (over one hundred degrees), so I planned to play golf earlier than my original tee time. That next morning, I drove to the Legacy Golf Club. Although this course was a public course because it was part of a resort, it looked much better than I expected and was like a country club. Since my tee time was not for another forty-five minutes, I had a heavy breakfast at the clubhouse restaurant, sitting outside under the palm trees. It was a lovely setting, and I enjoyed the meal! I thought to myself, *This course should be a country club . . . the amenities are absolutely great!*

I played with Dave, Tony, and Fred. All three were local guys, but Dave lived in Phoenix in the winter and in Chicago during the summer. The starter asked us to drink a lot of water because of the heat. By the time we finished our round, it was 107 degrees. During the round, I probably drank about a full gallon of cold water and made frequent stops in the restrooms. Although it was really hot, there was also an occasional breeze, which made it a little better. With the combination of drinking water and the breeze, it didn't feel like 107 degrees that afternoon.

I told the gentlemen I was playing with that I had been traveling and playing golf in different capitals. During the round, I played fairly well. I was not doing amazing but scrambling and saving pars. On one hole, I missed the green, and my golf ball landed in the fringe. I had about fifty-foot-long double breaking putt, and I made the putt. Tony remarked, "Ben is playing too much golf."

After the round, Tony and Fred needed to leave, but Dave and I sat outside of the restaurant on the patio, sipping cold drinks and just talking. I took some pictures with Dave in front of the resort and texted those to him. Later, Dave's wife came to pick him up, and he introduced us.

While I was in Phoenix, I also visited the capitol building and a few other places. The state capitol had copper paint on the top of the dome. I walked around the campus, taking everything in. It was still really hot, and I felt like it was hard to focus. I asked one gentleman to take a couple of pictures of me in front of the capitol dome in the back, and he kindly consented.

I also went to the MLB stadium. I parked just in front of the building and walked around the area. The NBA arena was just before the MLB stadium. They were impressive buildings in a lovely part of the city. The hotel was just around the corner, so it made everything easier.

I had a late lunch at the restaurant, took a shower, and rested for a while before checking out. Since this was the end of my trip, I needed to organize my golf travel bags and luggage. The valet service brought my car to the front of the hotel, and I sorted out my golf clubs, souvenir items, and luggage before driving back to the airport.

Arizona was another great state. Seeing miles and miles of desert sprinkled with cacti, Navajo Nation, and those small red mountains and cliffs was special.

My flight was a red eye from Phoenix to Charlotte. Then, the next morning, a quick flight from Charlotte to Washington brought me home safely!

Golf Course Name:	The Legacy Golf Club
Address and Website:	6808 S 32nd Street, Phoenix, AZ 85042 https://www.golflegacyresort.com/
Capital Players/ Club Contacts:	Dave S., Tony, Fred
Comment:	*"Wishing you the best this holiday season and many low seventies rounds next year. I am leaving for Phoenix this Saturday. Let me know when you publish your book about your golfing trips to all the U.S. capitals!"*
Highlight:	Seeing miles and miles of Arizona desert and the Navajo Nation for the first time was exciting. Playing in Arizona in the desert was also very special. Part of the course was green with small trees and flowers, but I could see desert and cacti too. The clubhouse and amenities were unbelievable.

6/16/2018–6/18/2018

Lansing, Michigan
Indianapolis, Indiana
Columbus, Ohio

Michigan "The Great Lakes State" – 29th Capital

The drive from South Riding, Virginia, to Lansing, Michigan, is just about nine hours and 585 miles (Routes I-76W and I-80W).

I left home at five in the morning. It was eighty degrees in South Riding. Then, just ninety minutes north in Cumberland, Maryland, it was fifty-seven degrees and chilly—but it felt great! Part of the drive was really pretty, especially in Cumberland, Maryland. Almost half of the drive was on a mountain ridge, which was all green and lush.

Typically, I like to stop every two and a half or three hours throughout the drive to stretch my legs, walk a few minutes at the rest stop, and go to the restroom. I usually feel fresh that way, and it allows me to be more alert on the road. Once I entered Michigan, I stopped at a rest stop. There was a big blue sign with "Welcome to Pure Michigan." This sign/license plate came out after they had a huge water issue in Flint, Michigan. In total, I made three stops before getting to the golf course in Lansing.

About an hour before arriving, there was a heavy storm. Of course, traffic was a mess, but the rain was only on that part of highway.

There were new and old addresses on the golf course's website, which was confusing. I was having a little difficulty getting there from the address I had, but finally, I arrived. I parked my car further away from other cars and changed shirts in the back seat. Then, I went to the clubhouse and checked in.

A twosome was about to start, and I joined them. The club even asked me to pay later since those two other guys had just teed off, and they wanted me to join them since I had to play with somebody. So I joined Darrell and Rodney. They were very easygoing and funny guys. I played with them on the front nine. During the round, while in a photo-worthy setting, we also took group selfies. After the round, they took my pictures in front of the clubhouse, and I texted our group photos to them. All in all, I played fairly well. On one par three hole, I almost made a hole in one (ace) but missed by a couple of inches. Before they left, I invited them to come to D.C.

On the back nine, I played with Robert and Bill, a father and son. They were friendly people. Bill was in college and was a long hitter and a great player! They told me that Bill had shot an eagle a few holes earlier. I had one birdie when I played with them, but I played really well with them overall.

Since I had started playing immediately after I arrived at the golf course, I paid for my round as well as for some souvenir items after I finished. They didn't have many souvenirs at the clubhouse, but I bought whatever they had. Afterward, I sat down outside in their sitting area and had a drink. It was really hot, so sitting down, enjoying the view of the course, and relaxing felt great!

I also texted my friend Rajan to find out whether his nephew was at Lansing or somewhere in Michigan. If he was, I wanted to meet him while I was there. However, I found out he was not in the area.

From the golf course, I drove to downtown Lansing and the capitol area, where I walked around. I enjoyed the city!

After that, I checked in at the hotel. A few restaurants were close by, so I went to one and had dinner. There was a Walmart near the Marriott, so I went there and bought some souvenir items. I also bought a few Michigan State basketball jerseys and T-shirts for my son, AJ. In addition, I bought some for myself and also purchased some Michigan souvenir items for home. It was a low-key end to this wonderful first leg of my trip!

Golf Course Name:	Groesbeck Golf Course
Address and Website:	1600 Ormond, Lansing, MI 48906 https://www.groesbeckgolfcourse.com/
Capital Players/ Club Contacts:	Rodney and Darrell, Robert and Bill
Comment:	*"Congrats on playing all the courses. Thanks for the update."*
Highlight:	Playing with Rodney, Darrell, Robert, and Bill was special! I also loved the drive to Michigan, particularly driving through Cumberland, Maryland.

INDIANA "HOOSIER STATE" – 30TH CAPITAL

From Lansing, Michigan, to Indianapolis, Indiana, it is about a four-hour and 250-mile drive (Route I-69 South).

I left early in the morning from the hotel to go to Indiana from Michigan. I was really looking forward to being back in Indiana and Terre Haute since Nora and I had lived there from August 1989 to June 1990.

Driving on highways from Michigan to Indiana was not particularly beautiful but not that bad either. The entire way, I was looking forward to going to Terre Haute.

First, I drove to Eagle Creek Golf Club. I let them know my tee time, paid the green fee, and checked in. Then, I joined Brian and Tom. The temperature was about one hundred degrees, so it was certainly hot that afternoon. It even felt like my eyes were blurry a few times because of the heat.

This golf club had two courses. I believe I paid for the better course, but I ended up playing on their second course, which was not too much worse for wear. In terms of playing, I didn't have a stellar front nine, but I did better on the back nine.

We took a couple of group pictures at the course. After the round, Tom and Brian signed my golf shirt, and they also wanted to take pictures holding it. Those guys were fun to play with, and I texted those group photos to them. Finally, I bought the golf club's logo golf shirt, a hat, and a few other items.

After golf, I drove to downtown Indianapolis. When Nora and I lived in Terre Haute, Indiana (about eighty miles southwest of Indianapolis), we had visited the city of Indianapolis a few times before. But the city's infrastructure and the downtown area were a lot bigger than twenty-nine years before. Indianapolis looked clean and very pretty!

Then, I drove to Terre Haute, which was about an hour away driving on Route 70 West. Believe it or not, Route 70 started from the edge of Indianapolis. This was a little surprising but at the same time very convenient—I didn't have to drive far to get to a major highway.

After twenty-nine years, Terre Haute looked much bigger and busier. There were vast roads and highways passing through now. I went to the courthouse, Indiana State University, and our apartment where we once lived. That apartment was so nice and lovely in a quiet neighborhood. However, it looked like the landlord (a doctor) had sold the property to a lawyer because I saw a law firm sign in front of the building.

I also visited the public library where I used to spend time studying. Then, I went to the area where we used to eat dinner sometimes. As far as I remember, they only had Denny's and Chi Chi's as restaurant options. I didn't see Chi Chi's, so I stopped at the Denny's and ate dinner there. My favorite meal was the chimichanga.

It felt so great to be back in Terre Haute. Then, I drove to the hotel in Indianapolis. This downtown Marriott was very spacious! It was a comfortable spot to wind down my day.

Golf Course Name:	Eagle Creek Golf Club
Address and Website:	8802 West 56th Street, Indianapolis, IN 46234 http://springfieldparks.org/
Capital Players/ Club Contacts:	Tom S. and Brian M.
Comment:	*"This is Thomas. We played in Indianapolis, Indiana, on your capital golf tour of the U.S. I received your holiday card in the mail. It was great to see the picture of your family and read about your accomplishments. You did something really cool! Have a great 2019."*
Highlight:	Aside from golfing, my favorite part of this trip was rediscovering Terre Haute. Nora and I lived there from August 1989 through June 1990, almost thirty years beforehand. While I was back in the area, I went to see places we used to visit.

Ohio "Buckeye State" – 31st Capital

From Indianapolis, Indiana, to Columbus, Ohio, it is about a three-hour drive covering 175 miles (Route I-70 E).

I was staying at a Marriott hotel in downtown Indianapolis. Before I went to bed, I set the alarm for five the next morning. However, something happened to my alarm, and it didn't go off. I overslept, so I kind of had to rush in the morning. Once I was on the road, I drove to Columbus, Ohio. Since it was morning, the weather felt fresh and pleasant. There is not much to describe about the drive. It was mostly just a regular highway with some farms, trees, etc.

First, I went to downtown Columbus and visited the capitol. I was able to find a parking spot pretty much right in front of the capitol building. It was in the middle of the city and on higher ground. It was a sunny day, so the capitol as well as the city looked very pretty. I walked around in the mall area and through the city. It was an enjoyable time!

From there, I drove to the golf course. The clubhouse was not that impressive, but the course was pretty! I paid the green fee and joined James and Justin on the front nine. In the morning, it was not hot because it had rained heavily the night before, and the course was still pretty wet. Justin had just started playing golf, but he was still doing okay. The pair only played nine holes, so after the round, I stayed with them at the clubhouse and enjoyed some snacks and a drink. Both of them were super nice and fun guys! We had taken a couple of selfies earlier, so I sent them their pictures before saying bye and going to play the back nine.

As I began playing the back nine alone, the temperature started rising rapidly, so I began to drink a lot of water. On hole eleven, I saw someone was coming from hole ten, so I waited a few minutes. Then, Greg joined me. He said he was a member there, and he informed me that this course used to be a country club. Greg played fairly well on most of the holes, but he had some bad holes too. That happens in golf. He said he was retired now, but he used to work for a company that was my employer's competitor. He said when he comes to the D.C. area, he will give me a call. We took a picture together, and I sent it to him. Before leaving the clubhouse, I bought a few golf course logo golf items.

Golf Course Name:	Championships Golf Course
Address and Website:	3900 Westerville Road, Columbus, OH 43224 https://crpdgolf.com/champions_course/
Capital Players/ Club Contacts:	James, Justin, and Jim
Comment:	*"Congrats on completing your journey! Happy holidays!!"*
Highlight:	The capitol dome is not really like a dome; it is different but still decent looking. The capitol campus was in the middle of the city, so it was not spacious but was still lovely. The city of Columbus looked pretty. A few holes on the golf course were pretty, but what was most important was that James and Justin were easygoing and great guys! Jim was also a very polite and friendly person.

7/3/2018–7/9/2018

Austin, Texas
Baton Rouge, Louisiana
Jackson, Mississippi
Little Rock, Arkansas
Oklahoma City, Oklahoma
Jefferson City, Missouri
Topeka, Kansas

Texas "Friendship State" – 32nd Capital

I had a connecting flight from Washington, D.C., to Houston to Austin, Texas, in the early afternoon on United Airlines. But at the airport, they changed my ticket and put me on a direct flight to Austin. They also gave me a first-class seat. Since I was saving almost four hours, I had to reschedule some of my plans, but I was very happy, as it worked out much better for me.

It was summertime, so it wouldn't get dark until 9:00 p.m. Once I landed at the Austin airport, I got in my car, and instead of going to the hotel, I went straight to the golf course. It was only 3:00 p.m., so I had a lot of daylight left.

I had my tee time scheduled for the next morning. Once I arrived, I spoke with the pro shop to see if I could play that day instead of the next day as scheduled and checked in. I also let them know that I needed to play with someone there. I waited for a while and found a single player, Jeremy.

We introduced ourselves, and I played the front nine with Jeremy, who responded favorably when I told him why I was in Austin. Then, Jeremy said this golf course had a lot of great history and also used to be a country club. We took pictures, which I later texted to him, and after the round, he signed my golf shirt. I enjoyed my time spent with Jeremy.

Then, on the back nine, I joined Roy and Mike—extremely kind older gentlemen! Mike was assistant director at the University of Texas. We played in 113 heat index—super hot! But I continued to drink a lot of water. Of course, we took our group pictures, and I texted those to them after the round. They also signed my golf shirt.

Looking out at the golf course, I started imagining that it could look pretty in the springtime with all the greenery. All in all, I played some good golf that day. I had more than five or six drives over 270 yards, so I was hitting well. My iron shots were not as decent as the driver, but I was chipping and putting better to save pars.

After the round, I went back to the pro shop to buy a few things. To my surprise, they already knew why I was at their golf course. I guess before Jeremy had left, he had let them know about me. I bought a few items and stayed there for a little bit. The pro shop gentleman was very friendly. He thanked me for coming to their course and playing, and he also asked me about my golf and traveling.

From the golf course, I went to the capitol building, which was huge and very pretty. I remembered when I met a husband and his wife in Charleston, West Virginia, they had mentioned how big and beautiful the Texas capitol building was. Yes, indeed, it was an impressive sight. I walked around the city, enjoying the environment. I also stopped at the souvenir shop and bought a coffee mug, magnet, etc., before leaving.

I had been to Texas once before. In June 2014, I surprised AJ with a pair of NBA Finals tickets to see the San Antonio Spurs against Miami Heat. In addition to our local teams, we are also Spurs fans. We flew to San Antonio to watch the first game, but we also stayed a couple of days for visting the Alamo, the River Walk, and downtown Austin. One day, we also went to Houston where we explored Space Center Houston, the Astros stadium, and the city overall. That was a great memory to reflect on while I was in Texas.

Golf Course Name:	Riverside Golf Course
Address and Website:	1020 Grove Blvd., Austin, TX 78744 http://www.riverside-gc.com/
Capital Players/ Club Contacts:	Jeremy S., Mike W., and Roy H.
Comment:	*"Thanks again—had a great time. Safe travels!"* *"Congrats—quite an accomplishment! Look forward to hearing your accounts of the venues/ courses and those you have met along the way."* *"Congratulations!"*
Highlight:	I most enjoyed the interesting history and information about the old original country club. Jeremy, Mike, and Roy were a great group of guys. The city of Austin was pretty too! Great, great capitol dome!

LOUISIANA "PELICAN STATE" – 33RD CAPITAL

From Austin, Texas, to Baton Rouge, Louisiana, is about a seven-hour and 430-mile drive (Route I-10E).

While I was driving from Austin, Texas, to Baton Rouge, Louisiana, it was raining really hard, and there were flashing signs warning "flooding" and "turn around if you see standing water" on the highways. Many cars had stopped on the side of the road. Visibility was low, but I didn't want to stop. There were some other cars with flashing emergency lights on, and they were driving slowly. I did the same thing, staying in the middle lane and driving carefully between forty-five and fifty miles per hour.

One truck was passing by in the far-left lane with a little more speed than most of the other cars. All of a sudden, the eighteen-wheeler drove through the standing water, and it splashed all over my windshield. I am not talking about just a little bit of water—it was a pool that completely covered my windshield. I felt like I had been thrown by a wave in the ocean. It seemed like I was submerged and couldn't breathe—it felt scary!

I couldn't see anything in front of me for seven or eight seconds but didn't want to stop the car. I feared if I halted or even slowed down, others would hit me from the back. So I kept on driving the same speed, hoping everything would be fine. Then, finally (yes, finally!), I was able to see again. Those seven or eight seconds felt like forever. It was very scary, but after that, nothing notable happened. It was still raining hard, but I kept on driving slowly.

I played golf at Santa Maria Golf Course. Although this course was in the Baton Rouge jurisdiction, it was outside of the city. Notably, it was designed by Robert T. Jones. Bobby Jones was a great player who also designed the Augusta National Golf Course (Masters) as well as many other famous courses.

I checked in at the pro shop, then found a single player to join. I played with Matt, who was a decent golfer. I had a great conversation with him. He was planning to go to Scotland with his friends to play golf, so he was all excited.

The course was pretty, and I played really well. It started to rain later on the back nine, but we didn't let that deter us from our game. The two of us snapped some pictures together, and Matt also took my photo with Virginia State Golf Association

(VSGA) and *Golf* magazine inside the clubhouse. I texted those pictures to him. Since it was July 4th, Matt gave me some suggestions about some restaurants in the city and where to watch the fireworks. Those were helpful recommendations!

At the hotel, I asked the concierge about the fireworks and the restaurants before returning to my room. This was one of the best hotels and views. It was not a Marriott or one of its properties, but it was one of its affiliated ones. I was on the highest floor. My room was absolutely cozy and spacious, and I had a breathtaking view—it felt like I was staying in the penthouse.

I took a shower and changed, then went downstairs and walked to the port. The entire street was busy, and people were strolling, making the most of the day. The port was filled with thousands of people, and they were all having a great time. That night, I saw a great fireworks display on the water, which made it extra enjoyable and pretty. After the fireworks, I meandered around the city a little bit. Either the restaurants were filled or about to close, so I eventually went back to my hotel.

I had heard this hotel's restaurant was one of the best. The restaurant section was closed, but the bar was open, so I ordered food from there. While dining, I met a husband and wife who were enjoyable to talk to. The husband had worked for the Arizona Diamondbacks organization from 2012 through 2015, but now they lived in Baton Rouge, which they loved. As a matter of fact, they told me that they'd had their wedding reception at this hotel.

For me, Baton Rouge was a surprisingly great and beautiful city! I explored the area by foot at night as well as in the morning sunlight. In fact, I walked to the capitol building the next morning. The capitol was cool, and it was very pleasant to stroll around the complex. Some of the townhouses close to the city were very pretty with the balconies in the front. So far, Baton Rouge was the best city in all aspects—the city, music, capitol, port, hotel, and food were all great!

Golf Course Name:	Santa Maria Golf Course
Address and Website:	18460 Santa Maria Pkwy., Baton Rouge, LA 70805 http://golf.brec.org/courses/santamaria/
Capital Players/ Club Contacts:	Matt S.
Comment:	*"Great playing with you. Good luck on your endeavor and safe travels! Enjoy the fireworks. Find a rooftop to watch them—maybe Tsunami restaurant on top of the Shaw Center if you don't have one available at your hotel. Have fun. Excellent! No problem. I enjoyed it thoroughly. Congratulations! It was great to meet you, and I'm happy you met your goal. And I look forward to hearing from you. All the best. Take care and thanks again."*
Highlight:	I especially loved the beautiful Port of Greater Baton Rouge and the spectacular fireworks display on July 4th. This is an absolutely gorgeous city in the south. The city, people, music, and food were outstanding. Even the hotel was one of my favorites!

Mississippi "Magnolia State" – 34th Capital

From Baton Rouge, Louisiana, to Jackson, Mississippi, is just about a three-hour and 150-mile drive (Routes LA-67N and I-55N).

When I drove from Baton Rouge, Louisiana, to Jackson, Mississippi, the weather was very hot—over one hundred degrees. I saw beautiful soybean and corn farms along the highway. Closer to Jackson, I also glimpsed a pretty river that made that area pretty. Mississippi is one of the poorest states in the south, so most of the houses and neighborhoods looked run down.

In Jackson, there is Jackson Country Club, and I was thinking of playing there, but I didn't have a tee time. Since I had already made a tee time at Live Oaks course, I decided to go to that golf course directly. Once I went inside the pro shop, I paid the green fee, but they couldn't print my receipt at the cash register. I let them know that it was important for me to have the receipt for a special reason, and I explained that even a handwritten one was fine with me. So they manually wrote a receipt on their paper receipt form and gave it to me. I thanked them for that! If I didn't need the receipt, I wouldn't have asked. They thought I needed it for a business reason, but it was for this golf journey.

Similarly, I needed to play with someone, but they didn't have that many twosomes or threesomes playing that day. They said Jim, a member, was playing as a single, but he had already started. I told them that was no problem for me, and I drove the golf cart to where Jim was. After introducing myself, I asked if I could join him. Jim gladly accepted my request.

Jim was a very pleasant person. We started playing, but shortly after, we ran into other players in front of us on every hole, so we began waiting a few minutes at each hole. As a result, Jim and I had plenty of time to talk about different things. I let him know that I was playing golf in different capitals. He was eager to hear about my journey. We also took a few selfies. After the round, we went to the clubhouse and had a drink. I showed Jim my golf shirt, which I had been taking to every capital. He was happy to check out the shirt and added his signature.

Part of the course was under construction, and the hundred-degree heat made it very uncomfortable, but I drank lots of water to stay hydrated. Chatting with Jim made it an enjoyable experience despite those downsides.

After golf, I drove to the hotel in downtown Jackson. Downtown was not that big. However, the Marriott was fairly large with glass windows all around. I checked in and asked a few things about the city at the counter. Since I was in the center of the city, everything was within walking distance.

After taking a shower, I walked to the capitol building area. It was not a big capitol, but it was very pretty with fragrant gardens and was located on higher ground. Then, I waltzed around the city. It seemed very quiet. Later, I found out most people in the area worked for federal or state government, so on the weekends, it was like a ghost town.

When I was done exploring, I walked back to the hotel and asked for recommendations of some restaurants in the city. The concierge gave me the names of a couple of highly rated places. Then, I started walking toward the restaurants. The eating establishments were a little further away than I anticipated, so I decided to come back to the hotel and eat there instead. This Marriott's restaurant was fairly large and had several things to order from the menu. Plus, they had big-screen TVs. I ended up ordering food there, and my meal was pretty tasty.

I found out later that pilots often stay at this Marriott. One pilot, I believe for Southwest Airlines, who was staying there got confused and thought I was pilot for American Airlines. He started talking to me even though I didn't know him! Then, he realized his mistake and apologized, indicating I looked like another pilot. That was a unique experience!

Golf Course Name:	Live Oaks Golf Club
Address and Website:	11200 US 49, Jackson, MS 39209 http://liveoaksgc.com/
Capital Players/ Club Contacts:	Jim C.
Comment:	*"Thank you for the great time. Hope one day to see you again. God bless you and be safe. Congrats!"*
Highlight:	Jim was an absolutely polite gentleman! I enjoyed the round with him!

ARKANSAS "THE NATURE STATE" – 35TH CAPITAL

I drove from Jackson, Mississippi, to Little Rock, Arkansas. The drive was about four and a half hours over 275 miles (Route US-65 N).

The temperature was about one hundred degrees, and the state looked pretty dry. However, alongside the highway, there were rivers and farms with soybeans and corn. The farms looked all green and pretty, which made this part of Arkansas appear extra lovely.

I also stopped at a rest stop along the highway. It was in the middle of a small town and by a beautiful river. This rest stop was unique with sitting areas and some historical statues and information. The day was sunny, and the river looked deep blue and very pretty!

I played golf at War Memorial Golf Course. This was a kind of military golf course. The University of Arkansas was just on the other side. I played with Dustin, Josh, and James, who were all friendly and pleasant to chat with. During the round, I took a couple of group pictures with them. This golf course was pet friendly, so people could bring their small dogs. One of the players had brought his dog, which was very cute.

Since it was such a hot day, I kept drinking lots of water. I played okay but not great. The course was a public course but not so bad. Sometimes, during hot and dry seasons, courses look a little brown and not that great. But as we all know, the same courses would look totally different in early spring.

When we were on the sixteenth hole, which was parallel to the road, it felt like we were literally playing on the street, and all those cars were just a few feet away. Strange but a different experience. Then, it started pouring rain on our last hole, so we stopped and went to the clubhouse. Dustin, Josh, and James came inside the pro shop and signed my golf shirt. Later, I texted our group's pictures to Dustin.

From the golf course, I drove directly to the hotel. This Marriott was a beautiful glass building with probably twenty or more stories. Also, there was a river right behind the hotel. I dropped off my car with valet parking in front of the hotel and grabbed my carry-on bag and backpack before heading inside. I checked into the hotel and went to my room on one of the top floors. From the window at the back, I could see a gorgeous view of Little Rock with the river and bridges. It reminded me a little bit of Pittsburgh, which also has three similar bridges close to the city.

I took a shower and then went downstairs to ask the concierge about the city, restaurants, and places to visit. They provided some information about where I could go and see different things. They also recommended that I try the Flying Fish restaurant if I liked seafood.

After exiting the hotel, I walked toward the right side. There was a walking path and a few historical museums. I also walked on the big bridge on the sidewalk. From the bridge, the view of Little Rock and the city was incredible. Then, I started heading back toward the hotel. The city was really crowded. Since it was Friday, I could see lots of people eating at the restaurants, walking, and enjoying themselves. When I saw people sitting outside and eating, I felt like I was in Europe. I also saw our former president's street name. Different parts of the city looked pretty and cozy.

I kept walking further to the other side of the city and spotted the Flying Fish restaurant. The line was all the way out the door to the street. I guess this restaurant was very popular in Little Rock. I spoke to a husband and wife in the line behind me who were from the area. When we were talking, I let them know I was visiting from near D.C., and they told me what places to visit and see in the city. They also gave me some advice on food choice at the Flying Fish.

In this restaurant, we had to stay in line, order, and pay at the counter, and then they would bring our food when it was ready. I ordered shrimp with a side and a drink. The food was great, and that's probably why we needed to wait at least twenty to thirty minutes. I enjoyed the dinner and the restaurant environment. I also took a picture of hanging art on the wall inside.

After dinner, I walked around a little bit more. The city looked like Thamel in Kathmandu. Little Rock was such a peaceful city and surprisingly beautiful. I enjoyed my time there.

Dustin got married a couple of years later, and I was invited to his wedding. Unfortunately, I was in Nepal, so I couldn't attend, but I wish them all the best.

Golf Course Name:	War Memorial Golf Course
Address and Website:	Club House Drive, Little Rock, AR 72205 https://www.warmemorialgolf.com/
Capital Players/ Club Contacts:	Dustin, Josh, and James
Comment:	*"Awesome! We had a blast! It was a pleasure. Okay! We were wondering if you would document it all in the end. I would love to hear about your whole journey. Very glad we were able to be part of it. One more thing, what did you say the name of your club is in D.C.? My grandpa has traveled for business and has played golf in many different places. Wanted to share the story with him and ask if he had heard of your club. That was an awesome day I will never forget! I hope all is well. Can't wait to hear about your journey."*
Highlight:	The city of Little Rock is by the Arkansas River, and walking in the city in the evening was very cozy and comfortable. Of course, I must also mention the delicious seafood at the Flying Fish restaurant.

Oklahoma "Native America State" – 36th Capital

From Little Rock, Arkansas, to Oklahoma City, Oklahoma, is about a five-hour drive covering 340 miles (Route I-40 W).

Driving from Little Rock to Oklahoma City was not particularly great, but occasionally along the highway, there were some pleasantly wooded areas, almost like a jungle, which made the scenery more enjoyable. Alongside the highway, I saw a "free restroom" sign that I thought was funny.

I drove directly to the golf course. It was a fairly hot day but sunny and nice. This was a public golf course, so when I arrived there and went inside the clubhouse, I originally thought I had gone to the wrong one. It was huge with two courses! I thought it was it was too good to be a public golf course but more like a semi-private golf club with all the amenities, course layout, etc.

I checked in and stated that I wanted to golf with other players. They said there was a twosome who just started if I would like I could join them. That was fine with me. I drove the cart and met Richard and Ricky on the second tee box. I introduced myself and let them know that the club had sent me to join them. They said that I could go ahead of them, but I said I needed to play with someone local. They happily agreed we could play together.

Richard and Ricky were father and son and very fun guys to play with. They were telling golf jokes, which were funny and made the game entertaining, especially because it was kind of a hot day outside. I played really well, and Richard and Ricky kindly complimented my game the entire time. We took a few selfies on the course, and after that round, they signed my golf shirt. I also texted them our group pictures. Before they left, I invited them to D.C.

Since I had started at the second hole, I needed to play hole one to complete the round. I checked at the pro shop, then went to the first tee box and joined another gentleman. We both missed our birdie putts, but the par was fine.

This golf course was one of the best public courses I had played—from the course to the amenities. Their clubhouse, the selection of clothing and other merchandise at the pro shop, and the restaurant were also just great. This could have easily been a semi-country club.

Garry was at the pro shop. I bought a shirt, a hat, and a few other things. I also bought a Titleist backpack, which usually costs about one hundred dollars anywhere else, for thirty dollars. Titleist products usually don't go on sale, so I don't know what happened or why they were selling this bag only for thirty dollars. But I was happy I got it and have been using it ever since. Titleist items are high-quality products that last forever.

From the golf course, I drove downtown to where the capitol building was. It was late in the afternoon, so the evening sunlight made the setting even lovelier. This capitol was also very big and beautiful!

I stayed at the Courtyard Marriott next to the Oklahoma City basketball arena. From the hotel room, I could see the convention center pretty much across the street. After taking a shower, I went to explore the area around the basketball arena and convention center.

After that, I went downtown, which was less than a quarter mile away. Downtown Oklahoma City was just beautiful. A lot of people were walking on the street and just having a great time. This particular part of the city was a tourist area, and I could see guests visiting there from different parts of the country.

I asked someone local for the best restaurant, and they recommended Crab-Town, so I ate there. This place seemed like a great choice for seafood. The music, environment, and food were wonderful. I was there for about two hours.

After dinner, I walked back to the hotel. The city was very busy. There were lots of people still out taking advantage of the warm weather. It was safe and pleasant to walk around the city. I enjoyed Oklahoma City!

Golf Course Name:	Lincoln Park Golf Course
Address and Website:	4001 NE Grand Blvd., Oklahoma City, OK 73111 http://www.okcgolf.com/lincoln/
Capital Players/ Club Contacts:	Richard and Ricky (father and son)

Comment:	*No problem. Hope you had a great time in OKC. Glad to hear that. We enjoyed playing with you and hopefully someday make it up there. Looking forward to it. Absolutely hope you are doing well. I think we might have won the best-looking group category lol. Merry Christmas and happy New Year to you and your family!*
Highlight:	This was probably the best public golf course I played in my golf tour. The golf course was pretty, but their amenities (pro shop, selection of golf items, restaurant, service, etc.) were outstanding. Downtown looked very cozy, safe, and pretty with all the tourists walking around—and the food was delicious!

MISSOURI "SHOW-ME STATE" – 37TH CAPITAL

The drive from Oklahoma City, Oklahoma, to Jefferson City, Missouri, is just about seven hours and 430 miles (Route I-44E).

The route was not particularly impressive. However, part of the drive was not so bad. It was mostly just regular highway passing some farms, woods, etc.

I decided to go directly to the golf course. My GPS was not working well, so I passed the road I needed to go on. It was just small one-lane road, so I had to drive about two miles before I could turn back to the right road again.

It was a beautiful day, and the course looked lovely. There was a putting area right before the first tee box. I paid the green fee and asked the pro shop whether I could join another group. There was a twosome starting in about fifteen minutes, and they said I could golf with them. A man named Chris—one of the players I would be playing with—was checking in at the counter at the same time, so I introduced myself. Joey came right before the tee time, and the three of us started playing together. They were great guys to play with.

All in all, I played well. During the entire round, I had one bad second shot (mishit) on par five on hole ten. Luckily, I hit my fourth shot on the green inside twelve feet, then made the par the hard way. Sometimes we can afford to have a bad shot on par five and still get away with par. Then, I had four birdies in the first seven holes. I was going to the seventeenth hole with five under, and it was getting dark. Then, I had back-to-back bogeys on the seventeenth and eighteenth holes and shot sixty-nine.

Chris and Joey were only supposed to play nine holes, but we had such a great time that I asked them whether they would be able to play the back nine with me as well. They responded, "When are we going to get another chance to play with Ben?" So both Chris and Joey called their families at home, letting them know that they would be playing a complete round. It was very nice of them to stay to play another nine holes with me. I told them that I appreciated that!

During the back nine, I noticed a cute dog, which followed us throughout our round. It must have belonged to one of the owners who played golf and lived on the course. One funny thing about that dog was if we hit the ball out of bounds (hazard, woods, etc.) or even on the rough, it would go get the golf ball and bring it back to us. If we missed the green, the dog would get the golf ball and put it on the green. What a goofy but well-trained dog! We all kept laughing and playing.

This particular day, I didn't have any really bad shots, so I was safe, and the dog didn't have to do anything. But Chris and Joey had a couple of bad holes, and the dog brought their golf balls back to them—very funny!

After the round, we went inside, and Chris and Joey signed my shirt. They also wanted to take pictures with me and with my golf shirt. We snapped some photos, which I sent to both of them. Then, they said goodbye and left. Later, I received texts from both Chris and Joey saying they had really enjoyed playing with me and hoped to play again someday. I felt the same way.

I bought a golf shirt, a hat, and a few other things before leaving the course. I had a really wonderful memory of the afternoon: Chris and Joey being awesome guys, a sunny and lovely day, the cute and funny dog at the course, and shooting under par round—all great stuff!

It was dark outside when I left the golf course and went to the hotel. I checked in at the Marriott and had a delicious dinner before going to bed.

After playing golf, I usually look at my scorecard twice to make sure I played in the capital golf course and included the names of the players who I played with as well as my score. So the next morning, as I was preparing to go downtown to visit the capitol, I examined my scorecard. To my dismay, I realized that instead of playing in Jefferson City, the capital of Missouri, I had played golf at Holt Summit, just outside of the capital, the day before. That was a big problem for me. If I couldn't play that day, I would have to come back to Jefferson City, Missouri, to play golf another time.

So I shuffled my plans. I went to the capitol area earlier than I had originally intended. I parked my car pretty much in front of the capitol building, which was being renovated. As a result, part of the capitol section was closed. I took a few pictures of the building and dome, then started walking around the city. That area was on higher ground, and the Missouri River was behind the capitol, so the city looked very pretty!

After the city and capitol visit, I went directly to Oak Hills Golf Center in Jefferson City where I had originally planned to play. The clubhouse was pretty. They were able to check me in as a single player, but I asked whether I could play with a member there. Tom was supposed to play with another member, but his friend didn't come, and he was happy that I joined him.

The course was pretty and kind of challenging too. In one short par four hole (270 yards), I almost hit the green. There was also one par three hole where the tee box was fifty yards above the green, and a pond nearby made that hole very pretty. I played fairly well but not like the previous day, under par round. Doug also joined us on the back nine. I took a few pictures with Tom and Doug and texted them to Tom. He also gave me his email address. After the round, I thanked both guys, and Tom signed my golf shirt.

I was wearing items with the logo of Eagle Creek Golf Club from Indianapolis, Indiana, at this course. When I went to the pro shop to buy a few things, the pro shop staff noticed the Eagle Creek logo. Then, she said she had played at Eagle Creek Golf Club. As I discovered, there is another decent course in Orlando with the same name, and she thought the golf shirt I was wearing was from there. However, I let her know that the shirt was from Indianapolis. I bought a few things, and she gave me some discounts. Then, I left the golf course. What a wild ride, but I was able to accomplish the Jefferson City leg of my journey without too much trouble.

Golf Course Name:	Oak Hills Golf Center
Address and Website:	932 Ellis Blvd., Jefferson City, MO 65101 http://www.jeffersoncitymo.gov/facilities_and_rentals/oak_hills_golf_center/index.php

Capital Players/ Club Contacts:	Chris, Joey, Tom, and Doug
Comment:	*"It's been a real pleasure meeting/playing golf with you. Heck of a story. I think it's awesome how you travel and play at different courses/ capitals. We will keep in touch for sure."* *"Got your Christmas card today. What a nice-looking family. You had everybody at the golf course guessing who would be sending me a card at the Oak Hills address. I was late in getting it because I was sidelined with back surgery earlier this month. Just the 'band-aid' type of procedure, and everything is going smoothly. Congratulations on completing your golfing goal. I hope you have a good 2019."* *"Really enjoyed playing with you! I hope we get to play again some time. Thanks for sending the email. Keep us posted about your travels and how you are playing. If you and our head pro play as a team in our league, no one can beat you. I got your Christmas card today! Thank you. I hope you and your family have a merry Christmas! Gotta ask . . . what did you shoot at Oak Hills?"*
Highlight:	Of course, playing at the wrong course the first day and coming back to play at the right course in the capital was funny but memorable. Playing with Chris and Joey and seeing that smart dog retrieving errant golf balls was certainly notable!

KANSAS "AMERICA'S HEARTLAND STATE" – 38TH CAPITAL

From Jefferson City, Missouri, to Topeka, Kansas, is about a three-and-a-half-hour drive covering 220 miles (Route I-70W).

The drive along this route was just okay. It was hot and summertime, so everything looked arid and not that attractive. There were not many pleasing views alongside the highways, but I am sure the dry weather and summer heat had something to do with it.

It was Monday when I went to play golf, and there was a golf league going on. I checked in at the clubhouse and asked whether I could join someone to play. Since league players were about to start in less than an hour, no one was playing around that time. I explained why I was at their course and why I wanted to play with a member or local. In turn, they asked those league guys whether I could play with them. One of the players from one group couldn't come, so I was able to join in his stead.

I was hungry, so I asked at the clubhouse whether they had a cart girl who sold food and drinks at the course. They said they didn't, so I bought a cold ham and cheese sandwich, a bag of chips, and a soft drink and ate outside on a bench in the fresh air.

Then, I played with John and Derrell. They were great guys. John was younger, and Derrell was a little bit of an older gentleman. It was over one hundred degrees, so it was really hot, but I kept drinking water throughout the round. The overall course was not so bad, but a couple of holes on the front nine were next to Shawnee River, and those were gorgeous. Since it was a sunny day, the river looked all blue, and that part of the course appeared very pretty!

I played decent—not great . . . especially compared to my excellent round the day before in Missouri. We took a couple of group pictures at the course, and I also asked John to take some pictures of me. John and Derrell mentioned that this course used to be a very highly rated and well-maintained course. I had a riveting conversation with them throughout the round. Then, afterward, John took some pictures of me in front of a fountain at the clubhouse.

John and Derrell only played nine holes. So I thanked them for playing with me and texted the pictures to John and emailed them to Derrell. Then, I played the back nine alone. I kept drinking lots of water to beat the heat. There were a couple of holes on the back that were also pretty! Before I left, I bought some souvenir items at the clubhouse. They were friendly people there.

From the golf course, I drove downtown. The area was not busy because it was the weekend, and most people around there probably worked for the state and local government. Then, I visited the capitol, which looked so pretty, especially with the evening sun in the background.

While there, I met a husband and wife and asked them to take a few pictures of me in front of the capitol, which they did. As I started talking to them, I found out that they lived in South Carolina now, but they used to live in Manassas, Virginia. Manassas is just ten or twelve miles from South Riding, my hometown. I told them I was from South Riding, and they knew exactly where it was.

After they departed, I walked around the city for a while. It looked small and calm but very pretty!

I drove from the city to a restaurant first. After I had dinner, I headed to the hotel. It was one of the Marriott properties, and the hotel was in another part of the city. The parking lot in front was full, but they had "Guest of the Day" parking available. I went inside and asked whether I could be the guest of the day and use the only parking available outside. They said no problem. I was happy that I was the lucky guest of the day!

My flight the next morning was at 7:00 a.m. from Kansas City International airport, MCI, in Missouri. The airport name is a little deceiving; it says Kansas, but actually, the airport is in

Missouri—Kansas City, Missouri. Since I had to leave early the next morning, I sorted out my golf clubs and packed my golf bag and put everything in the trunk. Also, I packed everything in my room before I went to bed.

The next morning, I checked out and drove about eighty miles from Topeka, Kansas, to MCI airport in Missouri. Since it was early in the morning, there were no traffic issues. I had to return my rental car, but I needed to fill up the gas beforehand. I tried to find a gas station alongside the highway about fifteen to twenty miles before the airport, but I couldn't find any.

Before you pick up your rental car, you always have the option to either fill up the car before returning it or to return with whatever you have left in the gas tank. If you pick for the rental company to fill up on gas, the price is just little more. But if you say that you will fill up the car and return it without a completely full gas tank, they will charge you up to three times more.

I always like to fill up the car by myself, so that's the option I'd selected. When I didn't find any gas stations until I arrived at the airport, I thought I was going to have to pay triple the amount of the money, especially because the tank was almost empty. But luckily, I found a gas station kind of inside the airport near the car rental place, so I was happy. After filling up the car, I dropped it off at the rental place and then took the shuttle from there to the terminal.

I still had plenty of time for check-in at the airport. After I went inside the terminal, I bought a big cup of hot coffee at the food court. I needed that so early in the morning. My golf trip in this region was complete.

Golf Course Name:	Lake Shawnee Golf Course
Address and Website:	4141 SE East Edge Rd., Topeka, KS 66609 http://www.lakeshawneegolf.com/
Capital Players/ Club Contacts:	John B. and Derrell D.
Comment:	*"Hope all is well and your golf is epic . . . Happy travels!!! Good to hear you've finished your grand tour of golf!!! Had a lot of fun playing around with you. I haven't forgotten to give you a call if I'm ever up your way for a round at your home course."* *"It took me a while to get over the heat last week but enjoyed your company and listening to your golf journeys."*
Highlight:	Seeing the view from the golf course of Shawnee River was very pretty! When I was in Kansas, it reminded me of the movie The Wizard of Oz. I saw this movie a number of times when Monica, AJ, and Serena were in elementary school. It was one of my favorite family movies, so being in Kansas was very special.

7
CONTINENTS

BINOD "BEN" THAPA
GOLF ADVENTURE - 7 CONTINENTS TO 50 U.S. CAPITALS
SOUTH RIDING GOLF CLUB, VIRGINIA, U.S.
OCTOBER 2011 – MAY 2019

50
U.S. CAPITALS

With 50 U.S. Capitals Players

With 7 Continents Players

7 Continents

Cheyenne, WY

Lincoln, NE

Bismarck, NI

Pierre, SD

Bismarck, ND

Pierre, SD

Lincoln, NE

Cheyenne, WY

Cheyenne, W

Bismarck, ND

Pierre, SD

Lincoln, NE

Salem, OR

Salem, OR

Salem, OR

Juneau, AK

Olympia, WA

Olympia, WA

Harrisburg, PA

Juneau, AK

Juneau, AK

Iarrisburg, PA

Harrisburg, PA

Olympia, WA

Boise, ID

Boise, ID

Richmond, VA

Boise, ID

Helena, MT

Helena, MT

St. Paul, MN

Richmond, VA

Richmond, VA

Helena, MT

St. Paul, MN

St. Paul, MN

Springfield, IL

Madison, WI

Madison, WI

Des Moines, IA

Des Moines, IA

Madison, WI

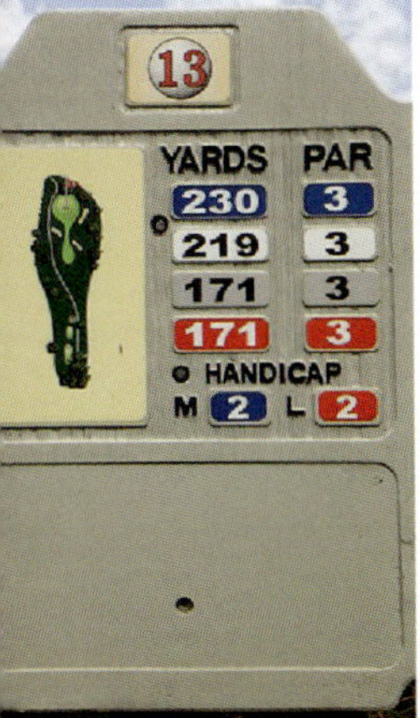

Springfield, IL

Springfield, IL

Des Moines, IA

Annapolis, MD

Annapolis, MD

Annapolis, MD

Dover, DE

Nashville, TN

Nashville, TN

Raleigh, NC

Trenton, NJ

Nashville, TN

Dover, DE

Raleigh, NC

Raleigh, NC

Trenton, NJ

Trenton, NJ

Dover, DE

rankfort, KY

Frankfort, KY

Sacramento, CA

Frankfort, KY

Charleston, WV

Charleston, WV

arleston, WV

Sacramento, CA

Sacramento, CA

Carson City, NV

Carson City, NV

Carson City, NV

Salt Lake City, UT

Salt Lake City, UT

Santa Fe, NM

Denver, CO

Denver, CO

Salt Lake City, UT

Phoenix, AZ

Phoenix, AZ

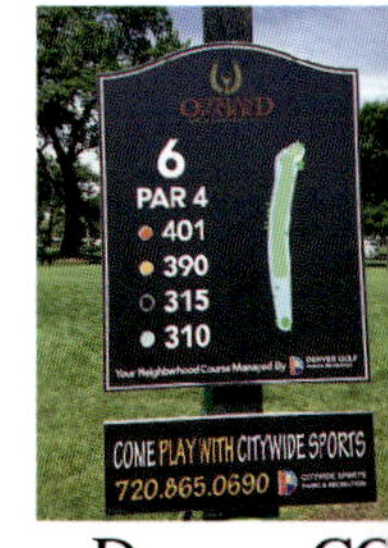

Denver, CO

Phoenix, AZ

Santa Fe, NM

Santa Fe, NM

Austin, TX

Columbus, OH

Austin, TX

ianapolis, IN

Columbus, OH

Lansing, MI

Austin, TX

Indianapolis, IN

Indianapolis, IN

Lansing, MI

Lansing, MI

Columbus, OH

Baton Rouge, LA

Baton Rouge, LA

Little Rock, AR

Baton Rouge, LA

Jackson, MS

Jackson, MS

Jackson, MS

Little Rock, AR

Little Rock, AR

Oklahoma City, OK

Oklahoma City, OK

Oklahoma City, OK

Topeka, KS

Holts Summit, MO

Topeka, KS

fferson City, MO

Jefferson City, MO

Holts Summit, MO

efferson City, MO

Holts Summit, MO

Augusta, ME

Augusta, ME

Topeka, KS

Augusta, ME

Providence, RI

Boston, MA

Providence, RI

Concord, NH

Providence, RI

Boston, MA

Montpelier, VT

Concord, NH

Concord, NH

Montpelier, VT

Montpelier, VT

Boston, MA

Atlanta, GA

Albany, NY

Montgomery, AL

Albany, NY

Tallahassee, FL

Tallahassee, FL

allahassee, FL

Montgomery, AL

Montgomery, AL

Atlanta, GA

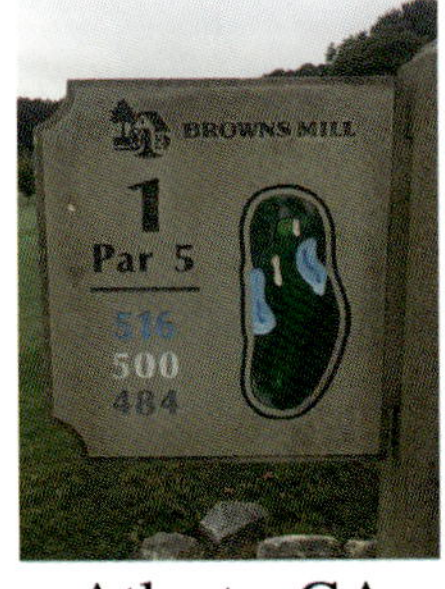

Atlanta, GA

Albany, NY

Honolulu, HI

Columbia, SC

Honolulu, HI

West Hartford, CT

Honolulu, HI

Columbia, SC

Honolulu, HI

Columbia, SC

West Hartford, C

Hartford, CT

Honolulu, HI

Hartford, CT

mily in Chichen Itza

2019 WNL Champs

Club Champion 2016

Canada

Family in Quebec City

esidents Cup 2022

Member Guest 2017

Christmas Day

Turks and Caicos

Thanksgiving

WNL 2019

Christmas Eve

Ryder Cup 2022

)18 Three-Club Champion

2022 WNL Champs

Both Parents

PC Team

North America

Mirage City GC, Cairo, Egypt

Mirage City GC, Cairo, Egypt

In Morocco with Monica and Serena

Mirage City GC, Cairo, Egypt

In Morocco with Monica and Serena

Giza, Egypt

Giza, Egypt

Nile River, Cairo, Egypt

In Morocco with Monica and Seren

Sydney, Australia

North Ryde GC,
Sydney, Australia

North Ryde GC,
Sydney, Australia

North Ryde GC,
Sydney, Australia

Sydney, Australia

North Ryde GC,
Sydney, Australia

Sydney, Australia

Sydney, Australia

Sydney, Australia

Australia

Paraguay

Uruguay

Bolivia

Peru

Paraguay

Beagle Channel 2013

Rio, Brazil 2013

Peru

Uruguay

Buenos Aires, Argentina 2013

Rio, Brazil 2013

Rio, Brazil 2013

Uruguay

Ushuaia, Argentina 201

Buenos Aires, Argentina 2013

Buenos Aires, Argentina 2013

Rio, Brazil 2013

Chile

South America

Sea Lion, Antarctica

Camping

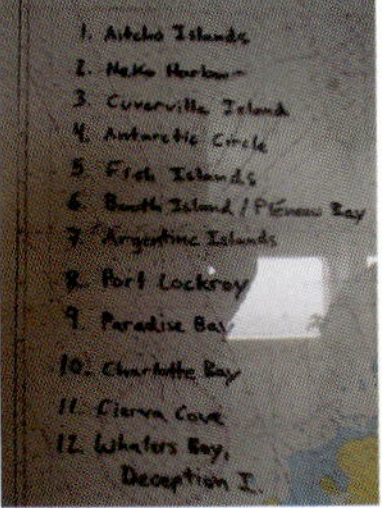

Antarctica

Kayaking in Antarctica

Binod in Antarctica

Humpback Whale, Antarctica

Expedition Staff

First Sunrise, Antarctica

urope Friends, Antarctica

Prospect Point, Antarctica 2013

Penguin, Antarctica

South of Antarctic Circle

Drake Passage

Polar Plunge, Antarctica

Writing Postcards from Antarctica

Antarctica

Parents

Philippines

Mt. Everest

Kathmandu, Nep

Nepal Safari

Parents and Family

Cambodia

Korea, DM

Grandparen

Vietnam

Kathmandu, Nepal

Abu Dhabi, UAE

Korea

The Great Wall
of China

Families

Mt. Fuji, Japan

Kathmandu, Nep

Families

Japan

Abu Dhabi, UAE

Parents and Family

Asia

Greenland

Paris, France

Málaga, Spain

Málaga, Spain

Iceland

Norway

Amsterdam, Netherlands

Finland

Málaga, Spain

Sweden

Vienna, Austria

Frankfurt, Germany

Sweden

Málaga, Spain

Málaga, Spain

Norway

Geneva, Switzerland

Europe

FNL 2023

FNL Champs 2016

Friends and Family

Friends and Family

Friends and Family

50 Capitals Player Autograph Shirt

FNL Champs 2016

FNL Champs 2023

FNL Group Picture

FNL Champs 2018

Friends and Family

FNL Group Picture

Friends and Fa

FNL Champs 2019

FNL Champs 2020

FNL Champs 2022

First Golf Game FL, 1993

FNL Group Picture

Friends and Fa

50 U.S. Capitals with VSGA

SRGC, FNL, Friends, Family, and Community

8/31/2018–9/3/2018

Augusta, Maine
Montpelier, Vermont
Concord, New Hampshire
Boston, Massachusetts
Providence, Rhode Island
Albany, New York

Maine "Vacationland State" – 39th Capital

The drive from South Riding, Virginia, to Augusta, Maine, is about eleven hours and 625 miles (Route I-95 N).

In Nepal, if we are going out of town, we like to stop by the nearby Hindu temple, especially if it is on the way to the airport or bus stop. Since Rajdhani Hindu Temple is not that far from our house in South Riding, I decided to go and just pray from outside before leaving. I was driving and approaching the temple around five in the morning, and obviously, it was still dark. Then, I thought about the security recording camera in the temple (these days, cameras are fairly inexpensive to install, and they are everywhere). So I changed my mind and decided to just pray from the street instead of going in front of the temple. Although sometimes we think we don't need to worry about these things . . . these days, we kind of do.

It was a weekday, so even at five in the morning, traffic on Route 66 in Virginia was moving slowly. Later, there was a crash on Nutley Street, so I believe officers only opened one left lane out of four lanes. It was about a thirty-minute delay. Then, I ran into some more heavy traffic on the Maryland side of the 495 beltways around 6:30 in the morning. I needed to drive 625 miles (1,000 kilometers), and I had already run into two traffic delays, so it was not a decent start for me.

But these two delays were nothing compared to what I ran into in New York City. Going toward Connecticut, there were a couple of fender-benders, and then the traffic was absolutely gridlocked. It took me two and a half hours to cross a fifty-mile stretch.

I wanted to go from Highway 95 all the way through Augusta because that highway runs from Florida to Maine. I had already driven south to Florida on Highway 95 before. So if I drove all the way on Highway 95 North, I would complete the entire route from Florida to Maine. But once I was in state of Massachusetts, my Waze app kept suggesting that I go on different routes. I probably should have set my preferred route from the beginning. I usually take the recommended fastest route from the GPS, but not this time—I wanted to take 95 all the way.

Even with all the delays, I stopped at a scenic area in Massachusetts. It was a sunny day, and I saw a big crystal-clear lake. All around it were trees and greenery—they all looked pure and serene!

Once I was in Maine, I spotted a corn farm. I also saw healthy trees alongside the highways. Part of the drive in Maine was just beautiful with small green mountains and beautiful lakes. There were a few rivers too, and the pure water made the state of Maine extra picturesque.

When I left Virginia that morning, it was fifty-two degrees. In Maine, it was ninety-five degrees and over one hundred degrees with the heat index. It was hard to believe the more I went north, the higher the temperature seemed to rise.

The sunset view in the evening looked very pretty in Augusta. I always thought Maine was different and unique, and it was one of the states that I really wanted to visit. Maybe Maine being all the way up north had something to do with it.

When I arrived, I went straight to the Marriott and checked in. In one day, I had driven through ten U.S. states: Virginia, Maryland, Delaware, New Jersey, New York, Connecticut, Rhode Island, Massachusetts, New Hampshire, and Maine. It was tiring.

After taking a shower, I visited the capitol building. The city looked lovely in the evening, but for some reason, the capitol dome area looked a little dark. I walked a little bit around there. Then, I went to Walmart to buy a few souvenir items. They didn't have exactly what I was looking for, but I bought a coffee mug, magnets, a kitchen cutting board, and a few garments.

The next morning, I drove to the capitol area again. In the early sunlight, the capitol as well as the city looked very pretty. I strode around the area once again. In the morning, I had a much better view of the capitol building.

I played golf at Western View Golf Club, which was the only golf course in the city of Augusta, Maine. I checked in at the pro shop and asked them whether I could play with some members there. One group had five players—all members—so I couldn't join them. But another group was about to start, and they had only three players. The pro shop said I could join them.

This group was about to start at the tee box. I introduced myself to them, and we began playing. Their names were Aaron, Jim, and Ken. They were not members but local guys. As usual, I took a few selfies with them.

It was a beautiful, sunny morning. Since it was a nine-hole course, we had to play twice to make the complete round. Mostly I played fairly well. At one point, Jim said to his friend, "This guy is like a pro," referring to me. The course was decent, but the trees around the course and actually playing in Maine felt very special!

After the round, Aaron, Jim, and Ken signed my golf shirt. Then, I said bye to those guys and went inside the clubhouse where I bought a few golf course souvenirs. I also ordered a club sandwich and a Coke. Then, I went outside and took a few pictures of the golf course near the first tee box that was painted a red color. I also took a few pictures just outside of the beautiful view with trees and small mountains—it felt pure!

Golf Course Name:	Western View Golf Club
Address and Website:	130 Bolton Hill Rd., Augusta, ME 04330 http://westernviewgolfcourse.com/
Capital Players/ Club Contacts:	Aaron, Jim, Ken T., Pro Shop Pete
Comment:	*"This guy is like a pro." "Very cool!"*
Highlight:	Maine is beautiful! It felt like I was on the top of the Northern Hemisphere. Everything about it felt very pure.

Vermont "Green Mountain State" – 40th Capital

From Augusta, Maine, to Montpelier, Vermont, is about a four-hour drive covering 180 miles (Route US-2 W).

When driving from Augusta to Vermont, I passed through New Hampshire. Driving through Maine, New Hampshire, and Vermont was just beautiful—all greenery, lakes, and beautiful mountain ridges. Just breathtaking!

I stopped at a rest stop that was very nice and clean. It was alongside the highway but was in the mountains. Behind the rest stop, there were two big flags (U.S. and state) on poles over thirty feet tall. From there, the view of the mountain ridges, one after another, was just gorgeous! I sat down there for a while and enjoyed the beautiful scenery.

From there, I drove directly to the golf course. However, getting there was not that easy because of the small and winding roads. I began to worry I wouldn't be able to play eighteen holes because it was later in the afternoon. Due to the mountains in the north, it would get darker earlier than in southern states, even though it was summer.

When I parked in the parking lot at the golf course, I saw some golfers still playing, so I knew I would be able to play. I took my travel golf bag and started walking toward the pro shop. Since it was a country club, I could see all the members enjoying, drinking, and sitting outside after their rounds. I talked to them briefly and asked them about the pro shop. These guys were very friendly! I also let them know that I had come to play golf as part of a quest to play in every capital.

Since one part of the pro shop was closed, I went to the bar section and paid the green fee, and someone else brought the golf cart for me. By the time I got to the tee box, a member named Kelly had arrived there. She said she had heard that I'd come to play golf at their club as part of my journey to play golf in every capital. I said yes, and she asked me whether it was okay to take a couple pictures of me at the tee box. I agreed! She wanted to share my picture with the other members and post it on their website. Kelly was a very helpful person!

This was a nine-hole course, so I saw two other guys come to the first tee box. I asked them whether I could join them, and they said no problem. So I ended up playing with John and Sampson, who were both members of this club.

I enjoyed the course. It was all green with rolling hills and was absolutely beautiful. After all, it was Vermont. What else would I expect, right? I imagine this course would look even more stunning during the fall time with all the colorful leaves.

I played fairly well. Sampson asked if I always hit straight in the middle of the fairways. I found out that John had lived for a few years in Massanutten, Virginia, which is about two hours south of our home. Our entire family went to a resort in Massanutten in 2003. We went skiing and exploring and did other things, but I also played one round of golf there. So we had lots to talk about.

I told Sampson and John why I had come to Vermont and picked their golf club to play at, and they both admired that my goal was to play golf in all fifty capitals. Sampson shared that, one summer, he played one hundred holes in one day. I congratulated him on that. That was unbelievable! I have played thirty-six holes of golf maximum in one day, so one hundred holes was quite impressive. He said he started first thing in the morning and played until it got dark. But it is still tough to do.

After the round, I talked to John and Sampson for a little bit longer and took a couple pictures at the course with them. Then, I sent those photos to John. They also signed my golf shirt.

After that, I went inside to buy a few things from the pro shop. It was already closed, and only the bar and restaurant section were open. I sat down with Andy and Patty out on the patio and had a drink. They were very pleasant people, and I enjoyed conversing with them. I also took a picture with Andy, who was trying to visit his friend in southern Virginia and help them with some furniture work in the winter.

After taking a shower at the hotel, I drove downtown and ate dinner at a restaurant. Once I finished dinner, I walked around a little bit in the city. Downtown Montpelier was kind of quiet but charming.

The next morning, I drove to the capitol building and walked around there. I took some pictures and drove through the city. It was a lovely trip overall.

Golf Course Name:	Montpelier Elks Country Club
Address and Website:	203 Country Club Rd., Montpelier, VT 05602 http://montpelierelkscc.com/
Capital Players/ Club Contacts:	John R., Sampson A., Andy and Patty E., Kelly F.
Comment:	*"What an accomplishment. I really enjoyed meeting you and hope to meet up in the future. The golfers' names are John and Sampson. The woman who greeted you on the tee box is Kelly. I hope you and your family are well. Happy holidays! The pro shop is closed for the season. They open in the middle of April, depending on the weather."* *"I hope you had a good holiday and happy New Year. If I am ever in the D.C. area, I will be sure to look you up. I would thoroughly enjoy playing more golf with you. I would like to extend the invitation if you are ever back up this way. I do not have an email address for Sampson. I will be sure to mention it to him when I see him."* *"Congratulations on finishing all fifty courses. It was a pleasure to be a part of. Thank you."*
Highlight:	Vermont is always my favorite state in New England. We used to go to Smugglers' Notch Resort in Stowe, Vermont, for vacation/family reunions. Stowe is closer to Canada, and I have played a couple of rounds of golf up there. I also climbed Mount Mansfield several times with Nora's family. So going back to Vermont felt great! Everybody was so nice and friendly. I enjoyed talking to Andy and Patty at the clubhouse after my round.

New Hampshire "Granite State" – 41st Capital

From Montpelier, Vermont, to Concord, New Hampshire, is about a two-hour drive covering 120 miles (Route I-89S).

The entire drive was just beautiful with small, green mountains and crystal-clear lakes. The roads were well-maintained.

I drove straight to Concord Country Club. I didn't realize until I went inside the pro shop that I had made a tee time at a different golf course. Since it was a country club for members only, I wouldn't be able to play. I let them know I thought I had called there and made the tee time, but by mistake, I had made the tee time somewhere else. Since I was already at this course, I didn't want to go anywhere else. Luckily, there were two members who were about to start in fifteen minutes. They asked me to join these two members—Mike and Les—at the 9:20 tee time.

Both Mike and Les were pleasant people. Les cracked some funny jokes, which made playing golf more enjoyable. Mike played especially well; his putting was really impressive. He would putt ten to fifteen yards outside of the putting surface, and he was really talented at doing this. He reminded me of my friends Dave and Richard from my own club. As long as it is dry, both of them wouldn't mind putting about ten to fifteen yards outside of the putting green—and both of them are skilled at it!

On one hole, I hit the ball in the water. Other than that, I played okay. I had only one birdie but a bunch of pars.

I took a few pictures with Mike and Les at the course, which was fairly pretty! Half of the holes were flat, and half were on elevated ground, so that made the golf more interesting and challenging.

After the round, I went to the clubhouse restaurant, called the 19th Hole, and had a drink with Mike and Les. I also asked one of the workers to take our group picture, and she did. I texted those pictures to Mike. Then, I invited them to D.C. and said goodbye before leaving the restaurant. The 19th Hole was all glass, and it looked so pretty from outside as well as inside.

Outside the clubhouse, in the putting area, I asked a young golfer to take a couple of pictures of me with the clubhouse in the background. I wanted to take two pictures holding a couple of magazines as well.

After golf, I visited downtown Concord. It is not that big but is a well-maintained city! It was very pleasant to walk around and explore. Everything seemed well-preserved.

I also went to the capitol building, which was quite unique. It was a regular building with a small piece that looked similar to a dome (but was not an actual dome) on the top. Although it was different, it was unique!

Golf Course Name:	Concord Country Club
Address and Website:	22 Country Club Ln., Concord, NH 03301 https://www.concordcountryclub.org/
Capital Players/ Club Contacts:	Mike D. and Les S.
Comment:	*"It was good playing with you."*
Highlight:	Seeing all the greenery, lakes, and beautiful parts of the state was wonderful. Concord was well-maintained and cozy! I loved viewing the beautiful green mountains and crystal-clear lakes in Maine, Vermont, and New Hampshire.

MASSACHUSETTS "THE BAY STATE" – 42ND CAPITAL

The drive from Concord, New Hampshire, to Boston, Massachusetts, was just over an hour and 70 miles (Route I-93S).

As you can probably imagine, the drive was very pretty. It was all green, and there were lots of lakes, which I could see from the highway. After all, it was New England!

I played at George Wright Golf Course. There were only two city golf courses in Boston, and JW Golf Course was one of them. It was obviously in the city but in an old neighborhood. The clubhouse was like an old red castle.

I went to the pro shop and just wanted to verify that this course was in the city of Boston. They assured me it was, and I looked at the scorecard as well to double-check. I paid the green fee and asked whether I could join anybody. They said no one was playing for next thirty minutes, but the pro shop asked me to check with the starter.

I was hungry, so I ordered BLT sandwich and diet Coke and quickly ate there. Then, I checked with the starter outside, and it didn't seem like anyone was going to play in the next thirty minutes. But the head pro was about to play. He said I could join him, but he also explained he was only going to play a few holes. As a result, I decided I didn't want to join him. I wanted to play at least nine holes with other players.

I waited another few minutes but didn't see anybody about to start at the first tee. On the tenth tee, there was a foursome, but I couldn't join them either, so I decided to play myself and catch up with the group in front of me. At the end of the third hole, I caught up with two guys—Preston and Nick. I asked them whether I could join them, and they agreed.

Preston and Nick were easygoing guys to play with. Because the group in front of us was very slow, we couldn't play at our own pace, so we went back a few holes and played them again. We also took a couple of group selfies on the course, and I texted our group pictures to them. After nine holes, I went to my car, and Preston and Nick signed my golf shirt. Nick also snapped a few pictures of me holding two different golf magazines.

Now I wanted to play the remaining holes myself, but I needed to return the cart by a certain time. Although I had already paid for the cart, I decided to walk the back nine holes instead. The starter dropped me off on the tenth green, and I walked from there.

I saw there were high school boys playing. It looked like a practice round for them, but I could see they were playing very competitively. They were hitting long drives, and their iron shots were impressive!

There were a few holes that were especially challenging as well as very pretty. It was hard to imagine this wooded area in this golf course in the middle of the city. I walked, played, and finished my round.

Afterward, I went to the pro shop and bought a golf shirt, a hat, and a few other logo items. I believe this club had hosted an amateur tournament the previous year, so they had some golf shirts with that logo on them. I decided to also purchase a shirt with that tournament logo on it.

After golf, as I was driving to downtown Boston, Waze took me through an old neighborhood, so I had to ask a couple of guys I passed whether there was a better way to get to the capitol. They said there was really no better route. They laughed and added, “It is Boston, and there is no way around!” I thought that was funny.

Eventually, I got to the capitol dome area. The city was all illuminated, and lots of people were outside, so it looked quite pleasant. However, it was also very crowded, so it took me an extra fifteen minutes to get there.

It was kind of hard to take pictures in front of the dome because I had parked my car on the other side of the street, and it was difficult to cross because there was no traffic signal, and the evening traffic was fairly heavy. Nonetheless, I took a few pictures. Later, when I checked them, I noticed they didn't come out that great, but the city looked very pretty and cozy overall.

I had been to Boston a few times before. Nora and I had taken the Red City Tour Bus (Hop On Hop Off) to visit different tourist attractions in 1990. Also Monica, AJ, and I went to the Red Sox game one year at Fenway Park and saw the Green Monster (a field wall in the stadium that is very popular).

Although Nora and I were married in Terre Haute, Indiana, in 1989, our actual big wedding ceremony with the family was held in Marblehead, Boston, in 1990. So it will always be a special place for me.

Golf Course Name:	George Wright Golf Course
Address and Website:	14 Earl Street, Boston, MA 02127 https://www.cityofbostongolf.com/
Capital Players/ Club Contacts:	Preston M. and Nick N.
Comment:	*"Enjoyed playing with you . . . very much appreciate it!"* *"When you play in Hawaii, let me know. I will give a couple of nice courses to play there."*
Highlight:	The city of Boston at night with all the illumination looked very pretty!

Rhode Island "Ocean State" – 43rd Capital

From Boston, Massachusetts, to Providence, Rhode Island, is about an hour-long drive covering sixty miles (Route I-95 S).

I drove from Boston to Providence in the evening when it was dark, so there is not much to describe. However, I had been to this part of the region and driven on Route 95 before. Since it was getting late, I stopped at a place to eat first. Then, I drove directly to the Marriott and checked in.

The next morning, I drove downtown to the capitol area first. I parked my car on the street and walked around the city. Parts of Providence as well as the suburbs were beautiful! There were some lakes in the suburbs and alongside the highway, which made Rhode Island very pretty. It was much lovelier than I had expected.

While I was downtown, I took a few pictures. It was fairly early in the morning, so the city seemed quiet and calm. The capitol dome was big and beautiful. Also, the capitol campus looked very pretty! I was not expecting this big of a capitol dome based on the size of Rhode Island. I took a couple of selfies.

Next, I drove to the golf course. I paid the green fee and let them know I had a tee time. For some reason, they had my tee time thirty minutes earlier than what I had asked. I must have written my tee time incorrectly. But they said my group was just about to start on hole two and asked me to join them there.

I drove to the second hole tee box and introduced myself, letting everyone know I was supposed to be playing with them and there was some confusion about the tee time. They didn't have a problem, so I joined Bob and David and started playing with them. They were local guys and friends who were very kind and welcoming to me. Bob has family in the Baltimore area, so I am sure I will see him again.

I played well except on one hole where I had a double. We also took a couple of group selfies at the course. After the round, I invited Bob and David to the D.C. area as usual. Then, I texted a couple of our group pictures to Bob. I also emailed a few of those pictures to David later.

After Bob and David left, I checked at the pro shop to make sure it was fine for me to go play the first hole because when I'd started earlier, I had begun at hole two. They didn't mind, and no one was at the tee box, so I played the first hole myself. Of course, I wanted to finish playing all eighteen holes. After that, I went back inside the pro shop to buy a few items. I purchased a golf shirt, a hat, and a ball marker there.

Initially, I thought I could order and eat lunch at the clubhouse restaurant, but I couldn't eat since I was still hot after playing the round in the summertime. Nonetheless, I had a cold drink, said sorry to the waitress, and left a few dollars as a tip for her before leaving the golf course. It was time and money well spent at a beautiful place.

Golf Course Name:	Triggs Memorial Golf Course
Address and Website:	1533 Chalkstone Ave., Providence, RI 02909 http://triggs.us/index.php
Capital Players/ Club Contacts:	Bob M. and David N.
Comment:	*"I enjoyed playing golf with you today."*
Highlight:	Although Rhode Island is the smallest state, their capitol dome was one of the biggest and was very pretty. Parts of Providence as well as the suburbs were very beautiful! There were some lovely lakes in the suburbs and alongside the highway, which made Rhode Island very pleasant. It was much better than I had expected.

New York "Empire State" – 44th Capital

From the hotel, I drove to Albany, New York. Part of the drive was pretty.

I went straight to Wolferts Roost Country Club in the morning. This place looked like a real country club with a nice cream building, a very pretty garden, and great landscaping.

I had contacted the clubhouse before but didn't have a tee time at this club. So I went to the pro shop and asked whether I could play a round of golf with other members there. I also let them know that I was playing in every capital and had picked this course to play one round of golf there. I had talked to one of their staff before, and he had instructed me to come around 10:00 a.m. They asked me to wait a little bit, and then they came back and said I could join Dave and Rob.

At the tee box, we introduced ourselves to each other. I found out that they were a father-in-law and son-in-law. They were super friendly people and decent players, especially Dave, who gave me some suggestions on different holes about how to play. Playing with club members is always beneficial for those who are playing golf at their course for the very first time because members play a lot of golf throughout the year. If the members are retired from work, they can easily play over one hundred rounds annually. That means they know the course well and can be very helpful to others.

The course was beautiful, probably one of the better courses that I had played in New England recently. We took a few group selfies, and I also asked Dave to take a couple pictures of me on the course, which he did. Since this was a country club, I believe on the seventh and thirteenth holes, they had small food courts where we could order sandwiches, chips, fruit, and drinks.

Dave told me that he had gotten a hole in one on hole eight, so I took a couple of pictures of Dave and Rob looking at the hole from the back. This par three hole was about 180 yards over the pond.

Dave hit a great shot, but his ball ended up one yard longer on the rough, and the pin was downhill—a tough position to be in. I hit my shot and was also on the green but about five or six feet above the hole—also not an ideal place to be. Dave chipped in from the rough, which was very hard to do from where he was. I missed my birdie downhill putt from inside the six feet.

I played fairly well; I believe I shot seventy-eight with two double bogeys for the first time playing at this course. After the round, we went inside the clubhouse and had drinks. Dave introduced me to his friends at the clubhouse, letting them know I was playing in every capital and New York was my forty-fifth capital. He also added Ben shot in the seventies with two doubles playing golf for first time in this course. His friends were very friendly. While I was at the clubhouse restaurant, I texted those pictures to both Dave and Rob, and they were happy to receive them. Dave told me he owned a company in Albany that had about forty staff members . . . very cool!

I invited both of them to D.C. They said they were coming to the D.C. area for business in 2019 and definitely would love to play a round of golf with there with me.

From the pro shop, I bought a golf half-zip winter jacket, which I needed. I also bought a hat, logo golf ball, and ball marker. Before leaving the course, I took a few pictures from the outside of the clubhouse and the garden. The blooming flowers in the garden looked very pretty, and the great landscaping!

From the golf course, I drove to downtown Albany. It was a sunny day, and the city of Albany, the capitol, and the surrounding areas looked very pretty. It was funny that when I tried to take pictures from different spots around the capitol, it looked better and better. The capitol building didn't have a dome like most others. It was similar to our executive building (the vice president's office) in Washington, D.C. It was very pretty! I enjoyed the city of Albany, especially the area in the middle (like our D.C. mall without the reflecting pool).

Golf Course Name:	Wolferts Roost Country Club
Address and Website:	120 Van Rensselaer Blvd., Albany, NY 12204 https://wolfertsroost.com/index.cfm
Capital Players/ Club Contacts:	J. David and Robert
Comment:	*"It was great meeting you."*
Highlight:	Seeing the city of Albany and the capitol building on a sunny day was quite memorable. It was a beautiful golf course, and the amenities were outstanding. Most importantly, playing with some of the nicest people, J. David and Robert, made my day.

9/29/2018–10/1/2018

Tallahassee, Florida
Montgomery, Alabama
Atlanta, Georgia
Columbia, South Carolina

Florida "Everglade State" – 45th Capital

The drive from South Riding, Virginia, to Tallahassee, Florida, is fourteen hours and 870 miles (Route 95 South and I-10 West). I completed this drive in one day.

I was driving from Jacksonville to Tallahassee, Florida, around eight in the evening on I-10 West. I was about an hour away from Tallahassee when, all of a sudden, my car started to make a noise, and I had to pull over on the highway. As soon as the car made that sound and the car began shaking, I knew it had run out of gas.

First, I was thinking of calling AAA for road assistance, but since it was a dark and busy highway, I first called 911 for safety reasons. Then, I contacted AAA for help. Unfortunately, I couldn't see any mile markers about a quarter mile both ways. Finally, I spotted an exit sign on the other side of the road that helped me give info to AAA. (For some reason, the phone was not showing me my location.) A police officer also came by to check on me, and I let him know I was okay and thanked him. AAA came later and put some gas in my car, and I was able to drive to the next gas station. All in all, I was stranded for over two hours on a busy highway in the dark.

Lesson learned—don't wait to fill up the car until you see the light! Fill up on gas as soon as there is a quarter tank left in the car, especially if you are driving out of state. (As a matter of fact, I was not waiting for the gas tank to get that low . . . I was driving in a rental SUV and didn't hear that warning sound.)

Even in this situation, I was thinking of whether my golf schedule would be messed up. Then, I drove directly to Courtyard Marriott in Tallahassee. Once I arrived there, I texted Nora and Serena at home, letting them know that I had gotten to the hotel safely. I didn't tell them about my car situation.

Even though this was a Courtyard Marriott, it was in the middle of downtown and looked like a regular Marriott—a tall building. I checked in and went to my room, which was well-furnished with a nice layout!

Since it was getting late and the restaurant would close within the next half an hour, I went outside of the hotel just to check what other options there were. However, either the restaurants were closed, or I didn't see restaurants close by. So I went back to the hotel restaurant and ordered some chicken wings and side dishes. I watched TV at the bar and enjoyed my meal. There were barely any other people because it was getting late.

The next morning, I spoke to the front desk and found out that the state capitol was just about ten to fifteen minutes away from the hotel. So I started walking to the capitol building area. I saw palm trees along the way. The capitol building and campus with palm trees looked very pretty. There was no doubt I was in Florida!

I approached a capitol officer who was very helpful and talked to me about the history of the state building. I took a few pictures at the capitol and then started walking in the city. The area looked pretty, and I snapped some pictures. Then, I came back to the hotel and had a filling breakfast.

Next, I drove to the golf course and checked in at the pro shop. I played with two guys, Nick and Christian, who were super friendly! Nick used to work at the state capitol, and Christian was about to graduate with an accounting/CPA degree. They had started playing golf recently and played whenever they could. I thought they played better than most people new to the game. I knew if they played regularly, they could improve, like everybody else.

It was a public golf course, so it was just okay. The back nine of the course was much better than the front nine. We took some group pictures. Both Nick and Christian asked a few times for some golf tips, and I helped them. I had let them know I was a member of a club and played a lot of golf. Since they were new golfers, I told them they would improve if they started playing more and figuring out the game.

After the round, we sat down at the clubhouse and had drinks. Nick and Christian asked me again for some advice for improving their game. I provided a few suggestions, and they were appreciative of that.

As always, I bought some golf souvenirs at the pro shop. Since I was in Florida, I called my cousin Samata and cousin-in-law and left them a voice message. They live in the West Palm Beach area, which is almost at the end of the state in the southeast. I was farther northwest and more than four hundred miles and six hours away, so I couldn't visit them, but I was thinking of them.

As I mentioned earlier, the first time I played golf was in Port St. Lucie in West Palm Beach in Florida with my father-in-law and two brothers-in-law in the summer of 1993. That memory was at the forefront of my mind the whole time I was playing golf in Florida. It was very special to me.

Golf Course Name:	Hilaman Golf Course
Address and Website:	2737 Blair Stone Rd., Tallahassee, FL 32301 www.hilaman.com/
Capital Players/ Club Contacts:	Nick M. and Christian T.
Comment:	*"It is great that you are playing golf in all fifty capitals!"*
Highlight:	With palm trees, flat land, and warmer weather, it felt like I was in Biratnagar in Nepal or in Singapore. It was very special to play in Tallahassee and remember the first time I ever played golf with my father-in-law and brothers-in-law in Florida.

Alabama "Yellowhammer State" – 46th Capital

I drove from Tallahassee, Florida, to Montgomery, Alabama, which is about a three-hour drive covering 215 miles (Routes I-10W and US-231N).

About twenty-five minutes before arriving in Montgomery, I started seeing bigger houses, and they looked magnificent. There was one house alongside the main highway on the left-hand side that was on higher ground, and it was the only house on the highway. It had a pool just twenty to twenty-five yards away from the road. There were no other houses for two or three miles. Initially, I thought that was nice, but then I started thinking having a swimming pool by the highway was probably not a great idea. Other than that, in this region, I saw mostly rambler houses.

I had called the Aroostook Golf Course a couple of weeks before to schedule my tee time, intending to play in the afternoon. I checked in at the clubhouse and, as usual, looked at the scorecard to identify the top first through sixth hardest holes in this course and mark them. Generally, I am a fairly safe golf player and don't hit many risky shots or take many chances, and because of that, I don't lose many golf balls. But I especially play it safe on the hardest holes. For the same reason, I play fairly safe on hole numbers four and thirteen because they are the two toughest holes at my home course, SRGC.

I played with a gentleman whose name was Shawn. He was an Air Force veteran and super nice person. We both played fairly well. I told Shawn that when he comes to the D.C. area, he should call me so we can play golf at my club.

Aroostook Golf Course was a public course but still was in decent shape, although a couple of holes needed work. We took some selfies on the course. Since Shawn was an Air Force veteran who was traveling, he said he had been playing golf in many places. I observed he was a decent golfer. He traveled to Japan, Hong Kong, and Singapore in Asia, and I was happy to hear he had been to that side of the world.

The pro shop didn't have that many items I could buy, so I didn't purchase many things there. After golf, I stayed fifteen to twenty minutes at the clubhouse talking to Shawn and the club owner, who took some pictures of me and Shawn. After a while, I said goodbye to them and left the golf course.

From the golf course, I drove to downtown Montgomery, walked around the city, and went to the capitol area. The dome and campus looked very pretty in the evening light. The capitol building was not that big, but other government buildings around the capitol and clean streets made the dome even more impressive.

Whenever I am in a state where I have family/friends, I contact them. Since I was in Alabama, I called my cousin, Suman, and we talked for a while. Alabama was special because of that family connection.

Golf Course Name:	Aroostook Golf Course
Address and Website:	1501 Dozier Rd., Montgomery, AL 36117 https://windcreek.com/montgomery/resort/aroostook-golf-course
Capital Players/ Club Contacts:	S. Lawson
Comment:	*"It is great that you are playing in all fifty U.S. capitals. I would also like to try something similar but on a smaller scale. Good luck in your travels!"*
Highlight:	Although the capitol had a small dome and campus, it looked beautiful in the evening! Montgomery and the state of Alabama have a lot of great history, so being there felt special. Alabama was also special because of my family connection and the memories I made in the past with family.

Georgia "Peach State" – 47th Capital

From Montgomery, Alabama, to Atlanta, Georgia, is about a three-hour drive covering 160 miles (Route 85 N).

Since I was going to be in Atlanta that afternoon, I texted my nieces and nephew, Sushmita, Smrity, and Rajiv, letting them know that I would be in Atlanta and could come for a late lunch if they were at their homes. Then, I called my cousin Manoj and left him a voice message, saying that I would be at Smrity's place for a late lunch, and if he was free, he could come too.

I left Montgomery early in the morning. The drive was uneventful. When I arrived at the golf course, I checked in at the pro shop, but they couldn't produce a physical receipt for my green fee. When I explained that it was important for me to get a receipt, they said I would get one, but it would be over email . . . and a few minutes later, I did receive the email. I was satisfied and thanked the staff there.

I played with two gentlemen, Harry and Terrance. Although this was a public course, it was actually pretty, especially in front of the first, ninth, and eighteenth tee boxes. This course reminded me of Gokarna Forest Golf Resort in Nepal or even my home course, SRGC. There was a pond, which made the course look even better.

Terrance and Harry made the round enjoyable. I let them know why I was there and explained that Atlanta was my forty-eighth capital in which to play golf. They were big fans of Tiger Woods (like many of us), and they mentioned that he had won his first tournament in five years at East Lake Golf Club, which was the last FedEx tournament of the year. Of course, I knew about that, and we talked more about Tiger Woods and how well he had been playing lately.

I also let them know that I had gone to a PGA Tour golf tournament the month before in Maryland where I'd seen Tiger Woods and a few other professional golfers just a few feet away. I'd also seen another PGA player, Kiradech Aphibarnrat, in between the ninth and tenth holes. At the time, I briefly said hello and congratulated him for great playing. Then, I showed Terrance and Harry some pictures I took of Tiger Woods and a few other PGA players in Maryland. They were happy that I shared.

After golf, I asked one of the staff members to take our pictures, which I texted to both Harry and Terrance. Then, I invited them to D.C. and thanked them for playing with me. Both of them said they were very happy to have played with me and signed my golf shirt. Harry also signed a golf ball and gave it to me, which was very nice of him. They were both great gentlemen!

The pro shop didn't have much, but they said they were getting some logo merchandise in a few months. Before I left, my final view from the back of the clubhouse was the first, ninth, and eighteenth holes with a pond in the middle—very pretty! I also took a few pictures from there.

From the golf course, I drove to the capitol building downtown. I had been to downtown Atlanta a few times before, but I had never been to the capitol, as it is not in the same place as the CNN Center and the Centennial Olympic Park. Since the day was sunny, the capitol dome and the campus looked pretty. I took some pictures there.

Then, I called Smrity, letting her know that I was leaving shortly and would be there in about an hour. Carl and Pinky's house was in a neighborhood not that far from Sushmita's house. I met the entire family there—Sushmita, Smrity, Marcus, Carl, Rajiv, and the children. Smrity and Carl's house looked lovely with plenty of rooms and a wooded area in the back. Their house was in a cul de sac with plenty of space for parking and a basketball hoop.

I had a Nepalese lunch/dinner at Pinky's house. I had been traveling and hadn't had Nepalese food in days, so I enjoyed dāl bhāt and great sweets. After lunch, we watched a little bit of the Atlanta Falcons NFL game together. Then, I said goodbye to my family members and left Atlanta to go to Columbia, South Carolina. On the way, I called Marriott to rebook the room in Columbia. I was ready for the next phase of my journey!

Golf Course Name:	Browns Mill Golf Course
Address and Website:	480 Cleveland Ave. SE, Atlanta, GA 30354 http://cityofatlantagolf.com/
Capital Players/ Club Contacts:	Harry J. and Terrance D.
Comment:	*I was hitting long and in the middle of the fairways most of the afternoon. Harry said, "Ben probably put something in the golf ball—that's why he is not missing anything."*
Highlight:	It was great to see Sushmita, Pinky, Rajiv, and the rest of the family. The Nepalese food and sweets were delicious! Atlanta probably has our second largest family group after the Washington, D.C., area. It was wonderful to reconnect with them amid my golf tour.

South Carolina "Palmetto State" – 48th Capital

From Cumming, Georgia, to Columbia, South Carolina, is about a three-and-a-half-hour drive covering 225 miles (Routes 85N and 26E).

I liked the drive from Cumming to Columbia. It was kind of quiet, and part of the drive took me past what appeared to be a wooded jungle, which made the trip even more enjoyable.

First, I drove to the capitol area. For some reason, being in the state of South Carolina felt good to me, almost like being in Maine. In the late 1990s, when Buwa-Aama (my parents) were here a second time, they drove with me and Rajan to Florida. On the way, we stopped in Columbia, South Carolina, and stayed there for one night. We walked around in the evening at a park with a lake in the middle of the town, which looked very pretty, and it's something I have always remembered. It felt great to be back in Columbia with those memories in mind.

Columbia looked beautiful during this visit. The capitol dome was not exactly like a regular dome but was very similar to the one we have in Richmond, Virginia. The capitol and surrounding area were aesthetically pleasing and peaceful.

From downtown, I drove to the Sheraton. After I checked in, I took a shower and went downstairs. This Sheraton was in the middle of the city, so I walked around a little bit. The hotel had a cocktail bar on the roof, so I went to the bar, ordered a drink, and sat down at one of the tables. I had my iPad with me and started writing about this trip in the notebook. It was a hot day, but at night, with the pleasant breeze on the rooftop, it felt much cooler and more comfortable.

After a while, I finished typing out my notes and went back to my room, which was fairly small but very cozy with nice furniture and a bathroom. Additionally, the bed had fluffy pillows, and the bed sheets were very comfortable.

The next morning, I walked around the city for a while. It looked lovely in the morning, and I took a few pictures. Then, I came back to the hotel and went to the sixteenth floor where they would serve breakfast. The breakfast was buffet style, and there was not a lot of variety, but overall, it was still pretty good. I checked out and gave my valet slip to the front, and they brought my car back.

From the hotel, I drove to the golf course. I checked in at the pro shop and asked whether I could join any members or players. They said I could, but I needed to wait about thirty minutes. That was fine by me. While I was waiting, I bought souvenir items from the pro shop. Then, I went outside near the first tee box. From the back of the clubhouse, the course looked wide and pretty.

Don, Jim, and Manny eventually came to play, and I joined them. After I introduced myself to them, I discovered Jim had moved to South Carolina from Herndon, Virginia. All three guys were friendly, and I enjoyed playing with them. I took a couple of pictures with them during our round.

Although this was a public golf course, it looked very nice. I would say more than half of the holes were designed well, and the course looked very pretty with a lake. Hole number eighteen had the course name carved into the hillside, which made it feel like it was a country club. I had played really well most of that round but had a few bad holes toward the end.

After the round, we went inside the clubhouse restaurant. Don, Jim, and Manny signed my golf shirt there. We had lunch together, and I asked a person that worked at the restaurant to take our group picture, which she did. Then, I texted those pictures to my three new friends.

I also met the owner and a few club members there. When they found out that I had come to play at their course and it was my forty-eighth capital, they said they wished they had known—they could have played with me!

After lunch, I said goodbye to Don, Jim, Manny, and everybody at the clubhouse and left. That wrapped up my golf tour in Columbia, South Carolina!

Golf Course Name:	Oak Hills Golf Club
Address and Website:	7629 Fairfield Rd., Columbia, SC 29203 http://www.oakhillsgolf.com/
Capital Players/ Club Contacts:	Jim, Manny, Don
Comment:	*"Good playing, good luck, and safe travels."*
Highlight:	This was a public golf course, but I thought it was better than the average public golf course. The city looked beautiful, especially at night from the rooftop of the hotel. The capitol dome was big and pretty.

10/28/2018

HONOLULU, HAWAII

HAWAII "ALOHA STATE" – 49TH CAPITAL

Nora had already flown to Honolulu, Hawaii, the day before and checked in at the Marriott there. But I had stayed in Kunming, China, the night before, then flew from Kunming to Beijing the next morning. I had about two hours in transit in Beijing before flying to Honolulu.

Beijing is eighteen hours ahead of Hawaii. The funny thing is that when I arrived in Honolulu, it was about the same time in the morning as when I had left Kunming—after two flights including a layover.

Once I arrived, I texted Nora to let her know that I'd landed in Honolulu. She said she was walking at the beach and asked me to text her once I got my car from the rental place. I passed through immigration, picked up a rental car, and texted Nora, letting her know that I was leaving from the airport.

It was about a half-hour drive to the hotel. When I arrived, I left the car with the valet person and let him know that I would need the car in about an hour, so I requested them to keep it close by. Then, I walked to the hotel lobby and spotted my lovely wife. It was great to see her in Hawaii, almost five thousand miles away from home.

My first choice to play golf was in two different country clubs in Honolulu. Since I didn't have tee times, I called those country clubs first to see whether they had any available. Oahu Country Club didn't have any open tee times, so I called Honolulu Country Club and let them know who I was and why I was in Honolulu, reminding them that I had communicated with them before.

Honolulu Country Club indicated they didn't have anything in the morning, but they paired me up with three other members in the afternoon. I thanked them, but it was only 11:00 a.m., and I didn't want to wait until 2:00 p.m. So Nora and I drove to Waialae Country Club where I had a tee time originally. This course seemed pretty flat but looked beautiful! In their pro shop, there were fairly big amenities on two different sides. Their pro shop and driving range looked great! However, for some reason, I decided to go back to play golf at Honolulu Country Club instead.

Nora and I drove on the island for a little bit. Part of the route to Honolulu Country Club was beautiful. It was Hawaii, so wherever we looked, the scene was incredible!

The Honolulu Country Club entrance as well as the campus looked sprawling and beautiful with a great sign in the entrance (something we usually see in Asia and South America). We parked the car, and I went inside. I needed to wait a little bit, but while I was waiting, I bought a golf shirt, hat, golf ball, and marker. Then, fifteen to twenty minutes later, I was able to join Ross, Debbie, and Lynn. Ross and Debbie were husband and wife. Lynn had intended to play with her husband, but he was not able to come.

The course was fairly flat. On one side, I could see the ocean, and the other side had small mountains, which made the course breathtaking. Usually, my rounds are better in flat courses like that, especially at country clubs. But I was not playing great, probably because I had just come back from Nepal after two weeks and I was still on Nepali time, which is almost sixteen hours ahead of Hawaii time. But still, no excuses!

I enjoyed the round of golf with Ross, Debbie, and Lynn—they were great people! We took a few selfies together. After the round, the three of them signed my golf shirt. Then, I texted our group pictures to Ross and said goodbye to them.

Nora is not a golfer and doesn't have that much interest in golf. However, she came to the golf course with me that day. But instead of driving in the golf cart, she sat in the outdoor clubhouse restaurant, had some snacks, and read a book. She said she enjoyed being outside and reading the entire time while I was playing.

We were staying at downtown Marriott. This location didn't have all the amenities like other Marriott hotels, but it was in the middle of the city and convenient. We strolled around the city, which was flooded with people just walking and enjoying themselves like us. The nightlife was vibrant. Then, we found a restaurant where we had a lovely dinner before returning to the hotel. On the way back, we stopped at a souvenir place and bought Hawaiian shirts and other items for our entire family.

The next morning, our Majestic Island Tour started at 7:30. We bought coffee and waited for the tour van in front of the Starbucks across from our hotel. I would say there were around fifteen tourists on the bus. It took us to various cultural and tourist sites, including Kahala and Diamond Head slopes; Hanauma Bay lookout; Halona blowhole and cove; Oahu's eastern shoreline; Nu'uanu Pali lookout; Byodo-In Temple; North Shore surfing beaches and Ko'olauloa Coast; Waimea Valley; and Historic Dole Plantation.

Every place the tour guide took us was just gorgeous. A few of the highlights from the tour were the absolutely huge and beautiful botanical garden, the beaches on North Shore, the view from Waimea Valley, a Buddhist temple in a very quiet area, and a pineapple farm where we had fresh pineapple juice. During the tour, we also saw multimillion-dollar houses up in the mountains. According to the guide, mostly movie stars lived in that neighborhood.

Most of the day was sunny and nice. We enjoyed the tour very much. On this trip, we met an older couple from Texas—a husband and wife, Jim and Trish. We had lunch and walked together on different tour stops. They were very friendly people. We took group pictures, and I texted those to them.

Next, Nora and I drove to the capitol building. It was evening by this point, and we had to park on the other side of the building. They didn't have bright lights around the capitol, so it was a little more difficult to see.

Nora and I don't fly on the same plane together, so she left Honolulu the day before I left. I dropped her off at the airport before finishing out my trip in Hawaii.

My friend John lives in Kailua, which is about ten miles northeast of Honolulu. We had worked together on the same project for about five years, but we'd been working at the same company for much longer. I had contacted him a few weeks before, and he had invited me for dinner, so I drove to John's house. Although he and I communicated regularly, I hadn't seen him in over five years, so it was awesome to see John, who introduced me to his friend. They served a special Hawaiian dish, and the food was great!

This rented house was an oceanfront property, and the value was at least three or four times more than similar homes in the D.C./New York areas. John said that they shared this house with another gentleman, who was a CEO of a small company. While all three of us were talking, the other owner came in, and John introduced us. We all talked for a little bit about golf and a few other things until the CEO, who had just come back from a long trip and was tired, said goodnight. I really enjoyed the ocean at night and loved seeing John again.

Afterward, I went back to the hotel and then went to buy some more souvenirs at a store nearby. I purchased a few things before returning to my room for bed. The next morning, I drove to the airport and returned my rental car. The flight was from Honolulu to San Francisco to Washington, D.C. I arrived home safely!

Golf Course Name:	Honolulu Country Club
Address and Website:	1690 Ala Puumalu St, Honolulu, HI 96818 http://www.honolulucountryclub.com/
Capital Players/ Club Contacts:	Ross, Debbie W., and Lynn T.
Comment:	*"Great playing with you. Thanks for the pictures! It was fun for us as well."*
Highlight:	I enjoyed playing with a great group of people: Ross, Debbie, and Lynn. It was also great seeing my friend, John, and enjoying his hospitality and the oceanfront home. There were gorgeous water views in Hawaii. One of my favorite parts was our Majestic Island Tour. Honolulu Country Club was the best golf course I played in the fifty capitals, probably something to do with the scenery. It was also the most expensive course I had played, but playing with great group of people on what I thought was my last golf course made it worth every penny! After I was done playing there, Nora said, "You did it!" Nora being in Hawaii was special to me! The fact that this was my last capital and I was completing my journey made everything exciting. We went to a number of places in our ten-hour sightseeing day. We loved the beautiful waters and beaches!

5/11/2019–5/12/2019

Hartford, Connecticut

Connecticut "Constitution State" – 50th Capital

The drive to Hartford, Connecticut, was decent but not like other New England states. First, I drove to Buena Vista Golf Course in Hartford. This is a nine-hole course. I paid the green fee for eighteen holes and waited a little bit to see if anybody was coming.

After a while, I saw two gentlemen with their twelve- or thirteen-year-old daughters coming to play. I introduced myself and asked them whether it would be okay if I played with them. They kindly agreed! Their names were Woody and Bob. The latter's daughter also played, and he was helping her improve. She played fairly well!

Overall, I enjoyed playing with this group, and we took some selfies at the course. Woody was a solid player, and he said he belonged to another country club in Hartford. At the time, he was preparing to play in the club championship the following weekend.

This course was fairly short; there were only par three and par four holes, but a couple of the par four holes were very challenging. The course looked fine. However, I knew it would look better with all green fairways and green trees in springtime. There were a couple of holes that had character to them. It was hot, but there was a little bit of breeze, which made it feel better.

One of the things I remember about this course was the par four hole nine. I believe the total length of this hole was about 270 yards, dog-leg right. But if we hit straight to the flag, meaning we went over the pond and small trees, the yardage was only about 240 yards. When I played with Woody and Bob, I went for the green and hit about ten yards longer, so my golf ball ended up in the bunker. For my second shot, I got out of the bunker but still left a twenty-foot downhill putt. Fortunately, I made the putt for a birdie!

Woody and Bob only played nine holes, so afterward, I went to the parking lot and got my golf shirt from the car trunk. They signed it, and we exchanged phone numbers. Then, I texted our group pictures to them.

After Bob and Woody left, I went back to play another nine holes to complete the eighteen-hole round. When I was playing by myself at hole nine once more, I went for the green again. From the tee box, because of trees and junk in the middle, I didn't see where my golf ball ended up. However, halfway through my walk, I realized that my golf ball was on the green instead of in the bunker. This time, I hit the green about twelve feet above the hole. I took a few extra minutes to putt because I was angling for an eagle. To my great joy, I made a downhill putt for the eagle. I was three under on one hole playing twice—that was special!

This course was part of the community and had other amenities. I didn't end up going inside the big hall. Overall, the place to pay for green fees was fairly small, and there were not many golf logo items to buy.

After the round, I drove downtown to the capitol building and walked around. Hartford's capitol dome was different from others. The top was painted a gold color, but the actual building was more like four squares. Most of the capitol domes are symmetrical, but this one is in the middle. It reminded me of the one in Dover, Delaware. The capitol building and campus were up on higher elevation, so we could see part of the city below as well as some residential properties up on the hilly area.

From there, I drove directly to downtown Marriott. From the hotel, I walked around that part of downtown. At night, the city looked pretty! What a wonderful trip.

I had to play twice in Connecticut. A few weeks after finishing playing my fiftieth U.S. capital in Honolulu, I went to my checklist and reviewed my documents to make sure I had truly played in all fifty U.S. capital courses. Then, I realized that the Buena Vista Golf Course was in West Hartford instead of in Hartford itself. So I had to take another trip to Hartford, Connecticut, to play at the Goodwin Park Golf Course.

I played the front nine in the late afternoon with Alex and Liz, whom I enjoyed playing with. I told them that they would always be a special part of my journey. After the round, they signed my golf shirt. Then, we exchanged phone numbers, and I texted a few group pictures to both of them. Later, when I was looking at my phone, I saw some pictures Liz had taken when I was putting and thought they came out really well. I sent them a text thanking Liz for the pictures! The next morning, I played the back nine with Joe to finish my eighteen holes.

Golf Course Name:	Goodwin Park Golf Course
Address and Website:	1130 Maple Avenue, Hartford, CT 06114 www.goodwinparkgolfcourse.com
Capital Players/ Club Contacts:	Alex and Liz
Comment:	*"That's good you are planning on playing in all capitals."*
Highlight:	Unique but attractive capitol dome and building!

Golfing on Seven Continents

In addition to playing golf in all U.S. states, I also had the opportunity to play golf in all seven continents. I played in Cairo, Egypt, Africa (October 2011); Parramatta, Sydney, Australia (November 2012); Buenos Aires, Argentina, South America (March 2013); Prospect Point, Antarctica (March 2013); Kathmandu, Nepal, Asia (October 2014); Virginia, U.S., North America (January 2015); and Malaga, Spain, Europe (March 2016).

NORTH AMERICA

SOUTH RIDING, VIRGINIA, UNITED STATES – 8/19/2000

Golf Course Name:	South Riding Golf Club
Address and Website:	43237 Golf View Dr., South Riding, VA 20152 (703) 327-6660 http://www.southridinggc.com/
Country's Players/ Club Contacts:	All members, AMC, FNL, WNL. Jon Fulton (GM) and Andrew Lester (Head Golf Professional)
Comment:	*I belong to this club. I started playing at my club in 2000, but I started playing a lot more starting in 2014 after all our three children started middle and high school.*
Highlight:	Meeting and developing relationships with all our staff members has been the greatest pleasure. They are all hard workers and great people! It's wonderful to get to know all members, AMC, FNL, WNL, and others in our club. I run Friday Night League (FNL) at our club, so I work and communicate with FNL players the most . . . It's a wonderful group of people characterized by great friendships!

I joined SRGC in 2014 and also got some help from the head golf pro, Chad, to fix part of my game. Since then, on average, I've played about forty rounds per year there, and I can certainly say joining the club has been one of my best decisions. It is not just about playing more—it's about meeting and playing with all these wonderful members and interacting with the very helpful staff. Put simply, I enjoy everything about this course.

My family and I were in Cancun, Mexico, in 2008 for about ten days. Cancun is known for its beaches, and that's where most travelers from the U.S. and Europe spend their time when they visit. (Interestingly, there were a lot more Europeans than American tourists.) Even though we loved the beach, we decided to do a few other things instead of visiting the beach the entire time. One of the things we wanted to do was to go outside of Cancun and experience the actual village lifestyle. But we also really wanted to go to Chichen Itza in the Yucatan Peninsula. This famous temple and landmark is a big tourist attraction and one of the Seven Wonders of the World.

Through the resort, we rented an SUV, which was fairly big and new and had a DVD player for the kids to watch movies on the road. The entire trip would take one full day.

Probably an hour after we left Cancun, we started to see villages and dirt roads. We spotted kids playing outside of their houses, some of them not fully clothed. Chickens and animals were just outside, and people were working in the yards or on the farms—very much like in Nepal.

Finally, we arrived at Chichen Itza. This place has a lot of history. We hired a tour guide, and he took us around different temples and historical places for the next two to three hours. Some of the history of the place was upsetting. But the place was peaceful like Lumbini in Nepal. Those few hours spent there were peaceful. We learned a lot and enjoyed our time together.

On the way back, we stopped at a village and spoke with some children and families. They were very cute. Before we departed from the village, we left some money for them. It was a wonderful experience I will never forget.

AFRICA

Cairo, Egypt, Africa – 10/16/2011

Golf Course Name:	Mirage City Golf Club
Address and Website:	Ring Road, New Cairo, Egypt Tel – 2409-1464 https://www.marriott.com/en-gb/hotels/hotel-information/golf-courses/caijw-jw-marriott-hotel-cairo/
Country's Players/ People:	Luzius and Robin
Comment:	*Many thanks for your pictures.*
Highlight:	My highlights were visiting the Giza Pyramid, going on a Nile River cruise at night, visiting museums, and playing golf.

I visited Cairo, Egypt, in October 2011 and stayed at the JW Marriott. Mirage City Golf Club was part of the Marriott, with the private course located just outside. Besides members, those who were staying at the property were permitted to play.

After introducing myself, I played with two gentlemen who were members of this club. The very first hole was just beautiful! Looking about forty feet downslope, we were greeted with gorgeous views! These two gentlemen were very easy to play with.

There were massive homes made of marble alongside the course. I asked one of the guys what the approximate cost of the homes were, and he said between 1.2 and 1.5 million dollars. It was 2011, and these were marble homes, so I actually thought the price would be a bit higher.

I played fairly well on this course. Usually, people play better if the course is a private country club because they are generally better maintained, and that was certainly the case here. After the round, we shook hands and said goodbye. I had a positive impression of the course and the people!

For all my trips, before I arrive in the country, I plan exactly what I would like to do while I am there. To start, I always co-ordinate and exchange emails with the hotel concierge.

One October 2011 morning, I was at the JW Marriott hotel lobby around 7:30 in Cairo, Egypt, talking to the concierge about my three-day plans. There were two guys behind me who were listening to our conversation. Later, as I was waiting for our tour van, I saw the same two guys and started to chat with them. During this discussion, I learned that one gentleman, Robin, was from England and the other, Luzius, was from Switzerland. When they found out about my tour plans for the next three days, they asked if they could come along with me. I agreed, and I was very happy to have them join me. The gentleman from England was a professor at the University of Manchester, and the Swiss gentleman was a high-tech guy who worked in Bangkok. Both of them traveled a lot. The job was easy for the English gentleman because his kids were grown, but the Swiss guy had pre-teen kids, so it was not so easy for him to travel.

On our second day in Cairo, we visited Tahrir Square, the museum, the city, and the Nile River, which runs south to north. About a week before I arrived in Cairo, there was a big protest, so we wanted to be extra cautious. I enjoyed sightseeing and visiting Giza Pyramid and other places with Luzius and Robin. I continue to communicate with both men to this day.

AUSTRALIA

PARRAMATTA, SYDNEY, AUSTRALIA – 11/4/2012

Golf Course Name:	North Ryde Golf Club
Address and Website:	137-207 Twin Rd, North Ryde NSW 2113, Australia https://www.northrydegolfclub.com.au/cms/ Tel - 61 2 9887 4422
Country's Players/ People:	Kim
Comment:	*You played really well!*
Highlight:	It was great to see Kanchan after almost ten years!!

In November 2012, I visited Sydney, Australia. While there, I played one round of golf at North Ryde Golf Club in Parramatta, where I joined a local gentleman, Kim. He was quiet and polite.

I started decently—the first hole with a par. Sometimes, when playing on a new course, it can be challenging, especially if it is out of the country and on a different continent. Fortunately, I played fairly well the rest of the round too. The course was decent. There were a few holes that looked particularly pretty. The clubhouse, restaurant, and amenities were very fine as well.

After the round, I returned my pull cart. Kim and I shook hands and exchanged phone numbers. Then, I let him know that if he comes to the U.S., he can contact me and we can play a round of golf at my course. With that, we said goodbye to each other.

In November 2012, I visited my cousin Kanchan in Sydney, Australia. Kanchan met me at the airport, and I rented a car.

Australians drive on the left side of the road, so it took me a little bit to get used to that, but I did fine.

I hadn't seen Kanchan in almost ten years, so it was great to be reunited with him. While I was there, Kanchan took me to so many places—the Sydney Opera House, the Royal Botanical Gardens, the harbor, the top of Sydney Tower, the zoo, the city and suburbs, and even the beach. While I was there, the weather was great. A couple of highlights were being able to see the koalas and kangaroos, but the panoramic view from Sydney Tower was just beautiful! Because Sydney is on the South Pacific Ocean side of the water and the day was sunny, it looked even brighter and more beautiful!

My uncle Mohan used to get very involved in the Nepal Australia Friendship Association. He also traveled to Canberra, Australia, in the mid-1980s. When he visited, he would bring some souvenirs and magazines back from Australia. In the magazines, we would notice the famous Sydney Opera House, the beautiful piece of architecture. I had envisioned and always wanted to visit that famous landmark in Sydney. So it was great to finally see the Sydney Opera House in person. I am sure in the last twenty-five years, Sydney and Australia have developed a lot, like everywhere else, but it was still an incredible experience.

Since I was visiting just for a few days, I couldn't see and comprehend everything. Luckily, I observe things quickly, at least at a high level. What I saw in Sydney was all positive. It seemed like a safe place to live with excellent public transportation and well-paid jobs. It was also a clean city, but most importantly, people could travel from Sydney to Kathmandu in just a fifteen-hour flight.

It was great to see Kanchan after ten years—we certainly had some catching up to do. I appreciated Kanchan taking me around!

SOUTH AMERICA

Buenos Aires, Argentina, South America – 3/9/2013

Golf Course Name:	Bunos Aires Gobierno de la Ciudad
Address and Website:	C1429 Buenos Aires, Argentina Tel – 4772-7261 and 4774-9158 http://www.clubciudadgolf.com/golf/login.php
Country's Players/ People:	Jose
Highlight:	Hitting a 159-yard shot from the fairway bunker to the green and playing partner and other groups clapping!

In March 2013, I visited Buenos Aires, Argentina, for a few days. While there, I played golf at a nearby public course. It's always good to make a tee time at any golf course (including public ones), but if you walk into a public course and they have openings, they will let you check in and play.

When I went to this course, I found out they had a golf tournament going on that day. I really wanted to play in Buenos Aires, so I started talking to the people at the clubhouse and to the starter. At first, they said I couldn't play because of the tournament. Then, I politely said, "I am from Washington, and I am in Buenos Aires just for a few days. Today is my last day here." The starter was a kind gentleman, and he understood my request, so they let me play as soon as the last group of tournament players went.

At that point, I started playing with a nice gentleman. This course was not great. Because there was little land (as it was in the city), it seemed as if the course was designed to run parallel. For example, hole one finished, then hole two started and came back from the other side next to hole one. This way, you would run into players from other groups on other fairways going in the opposite direction.

At one of the holes, I hit a bad shot from the tee box, and my ball ended up in the bunker. Per my golf Garmin watch, it was 159 yards to the pin from where the bunker was. From there, I used my 7 iron. I usually hit only 140 yards with that club (I swing only about 85 percent for better short game and accuracy). But I decided to use my 7 iron anyway because I feel comfortable using that club.

Preparing to do my best, I hit as hard as I could. It turned out to be a great shot. The ball landed just short of the green but got some good rolls until it settled in the middle of the green. All of a sudden, I heard not just a "great shot!" from the guy whom I was playing with, but I also heard clapping from the foursome that was playing the tournament and happened to be near my ball on the other side of the fairway. It was a kind compliment. Of course, I said thank you and tipped my hat.

Golf typically takes about four to five hours to play from start to finish. Usually, golfers talk among each other while playing. The guy whom I played with knew that I had taken a taxi to the golf course that morning. After the game, my playing partner generously dropped me off at the Marriott, which was very nice of him. We still communicate via email every once in a while.

In March 2013, I was in Buenos Aires, Argentina, for a few days. On the first day, I visited downtown and a few other places. There was a lot of construction going on in the city, but it was still good to explore places. The city, stores, and lifestyle had a very European feel. I heard a lot of people who migrated there from Spain and Portugal had an influence on the city's culture.

ANTARCTICA

Prospect Point, Antarctica – 3/15/2013

Golf Course Name:	None
Address and Website:	Prospect Point, ANTARCTICA AdventureSmith Explorations https://adventuresmithexplorations.com/cruises/antarctica/quest-antarctic-circle-travel-journal/

I was on the quest for the Antarctic Circle aboard MS *Expedition* with G Adventures from March 10, 2013, to March 22, 2013. The ship embarked from Ushuaia, Argentina. I had brought my 7 iron, yellow golf balls, glove, and tees from home in Virginia. In one of our continent landings at Prospect Point on March 15, 2013, I was able to bring a golf club and golf items. There, I had the opportunity to hit/swing at golf balls.

Day 7

"We were north of the Antarctic Circle. The day was cloudy, windy, and cold. After breakfast, the crew said they would do another continental landing. I was in the first group to get into the zodiac with about ten people. I brought my cameras and also the golf club, glove, and tees. I had brought these items all the way from Washington, passing through four airports. Even on the boat, I hid them because I didn't want the ship crew to tell me not to bring a golf club to the shore. They were pretty strict on what we could and could not bring.

Once we landed and they dropped us off, they said we could spend about two hours at the shore. But the weather could change drastically in just a matter of minutes in Antarctica. So I didn't want to lose the opportunity, and a few minutes after our landing, I started swinging my golf clubs a few times while looking at the beautiful view of Antarctica. One person asked whether I would like him to take my picture. I agreed, and he took a few photos I will never forget. I also took pictures of the beautiful scenery with my iPad. This takes much better panoramic pictures, so I was happy that I'd brought it along with me.

After I was done hitting golf balls, three or four people asked me to borrow the club so they could have the experience as well. They said they would just pretend to hit for the picture, and I was fine with that. They took a few pictures posing at a golf stand. Some people who were near the shore but couldn't get out of the zodiac because of the bad condition saw me with golf club hitting and swinging and probably thought it was a little crazy.

Not even ten minutes after we landed in Prospect Point, Antarctica, the staff members said the weather was getting really bad and we needed to go back to the ship. Our zodiac was the only one landed, and we returned. On the way back, in a matter of minutes, the weather got even worse. It started to ice-snow and became extremely windy and cold. Even the zodiac started to struggle to move in the water. Everybody was holding ropes with two hands, and some people were shivering and looked a little worried. I knew it was really bad, but on the other hand, this is what we had come down to see and somewhat expected. It was Antarctic weather—what we see in documentaries.

After we returned to the ship, we felt safe, and the hot coffee and hot chocolate made us warm. The same bad conditions continued all that day, so they ended up showing some more documentaries and getting us involved in other things inside the ship.

Some people said what a wild idea to bring a golf club and swing it in Antarctica. As a result, the talk of the day was golf. A few individuals came up to me and asked about golf: How did you bring the club? Why were you swinging in Antarctica? The questions went on and on. I told them I had visited all six continents and played golf. Even though we couldn't play golf in Antarctica, I still wanted to have the experience.

Later, one expedition team member found out that it was me swinging a golf club on the landing, so she came and talked to me. She asked me about the golf club, and I explained that I'd brought it from Washington through four flights. When she asked me whether they could use a couple of pictures on their slides, I gave her two photos.

The bad weather continued all day and evening. People started to watch part three of *Frozen Planet*. Then, I started posting day one through day six notes to families in WordPress. It was just one day of my Antarctica adventure, but in many ways, it was the most memorable.

Memory of White Continent

It's been over ten years since I have been to Antarctica, but it still feels just like yesterday. Every once in a while, I share about my Antarctic experience with my own family—bits and pieces, but there is so much more.

I always wanted to go to Antarctica, but I wanted to visit and see other continents before going there. In 2012, I was able to go to Australia, which was my sixth continent. So the last trip for me was to Antarctica. I tried to convince my wife to come along with me, but she didn't and couldn't. She cannot handle the big ship, especially this long trip, and Drake Passage's rough waters would have been extremely difficult for her. Besides, she didn't have an interest in going to Antarctica.

Before going there, I read many articles about Antarctica. I watched the *Frozen Planet* series several times as well as other documentaries on Antarctica and the *March of the Penguins* movie. After watching documentaries and reading articles, I would say I was fascinated with the White Continent even before actually visiting there.

My absolute desire and interest in going to Antarctica probably had something to do with me coming from Nepal with all the big Himalayas; over 80 percent of the country is covered by mountains. I was also kind of comparing Mount Everest being the tallest and Antarctica being on the bottom of the world—and the white Himalayas versus the White Continent.

I will not forget the ship's embarkation in the evening—cold, misty, a little cloud over the mountains, but just a beautiful setting in the back, the city of Ushuaia (Argentina). Most people were on the rooftop of the ship, enjoying the view, and I could see the excitement on their faces with the anticipation of traveling to Antarctica like me. The rocking boat in the famous Drake Passage and people getting sick was not pleasant but was a once-in-a-lifetime experience.

I was thrilled to see Antarctica for the first time. We could see small white mountains and icebergs. It was such a peaceful feeling to view the calm and beautiful Antarctica for the first time. To see my first sunrise there and make our first continent landing was special.

Buying a kayaking trip was one of the best things I did. I went kayaking six times and paddled more than forty-two miles in Antarctica waters. Hard to imagine! To see penguins, seals, and whales this close, we had to be lucky. Not just going to Antarctica but also going through the Antarctic Circle was memorable. People were cheering and laughing, happy as could be! Being able to swing a golf club for the experience was unique and bold, but I had to do it. I sent postcards to families and friends from Antarctica, and they took one year to arrive!

It was not a happy moment to see the abandoned research stations and museums, but because of the extreme cold temperature, most of these items in the stations and museums had been preserved for decades and were cool to see. Even though we didn't go camping overnight because of bad weather the third time, at least we put up the tent, and I was able to enjoy a few moments lying down inside of it. The polar plunge was so cold—and it was bold, but it was another once-in-a-lifetime experience. I enjoyed seeing the active volcano site in Antarctica.

After two weeks, when the ship returned north to Ushuaia through the Beagle Channel, it was a beautiful scene—sunny but with light rain and rainbows in the back. The water was clean and calm, and we saw Chile a few miles to the left and Argentina a few miles to the right with beautiful small mountains on both sides. Everything was memorable and pleasant—a once-in-a-lifetime experience for me. I felt like there was no better place on the planet than Antarctica!

Definitely I would have enjoyed this adventure of my life if my wife could have come. After the trip, I realized that about 25 percent of men who came to Antarctica were in a similar situation—their wives didn't want to or couldn't come to Antarctica, the same reason my wife couldn't come. They couldn't have handled the ship or had no interest in going to Antarctica.

Most importantly, I met so many wonderful people from all over the world on the ship. Most individuals would eat breakfast, lunch, and dinner with different people at one big, round table. This way, we got to know each other. I did the same thing—sat at different tables and talked to different people. All these people were friendly and helpful. They came right up and talked, sharing their experiences and stories. All of them were very friendly and polite. It was a pleasure to meet all of them. I still keep in touch with some of these wonderful people today.

ASIA

Kathmandu, Nepal, Asia – 10/8/2014

Golf Course Name:	Gokarna Forest Resort Golf
Address and Website:	http://www.gokarna.com/golf Kathmandu, Bagmati 977-1-4451212 My first round of golf at Gokarna Forest Club, Kathmandu, Nepal
Country's Players/ People:	Krishna NS Thapa and B. Poudel

I played my first round of golf at Gokarna Club in Kathmandu, Nepal, in October 2014. This golf club is part of Gokarna Forest Resort. My older cousin, KNS, lives in Kathmandu and is a member at this club. So when I was visiting Nepal, he brought me to play one round of golf there.

When I saw this course for the first time, I was kind of surprised and happy to see such a beautiful golf course in Kathmandu. The clubhouse was on the higher ground in between hole one and hole eighteen. Across from the clubhouse, I could see a fairly large putting green area that looked quite nice. From the putting green, there was a very pretty view, especially toward the eighteenth hole!

I played golf with my cousin and two of his friends. Each of us had our own caddie. I'd never had my own caddie before! When we play golf in the States, we usually have carts or sometimes we just like to walk for cardio exercise. My caddie was a very kind and polite young man, and he gave me some good advice, especially since I was playing on this course for the first time. I had a wonderful chat with him, and I also took a picture with him.

The course was mostly surrounded by woods and had some open areas as well. We saw a herd of deer crossing in the middle of the fairways and also spotted monkeys here and there on the golf course. I was not just enjoying walking and playing golf with family and friends—I was also very much enjoying the greenery, nature, and animals. It was kind of an adventure and such a great experience! Since the course was on higher ground, it reminded me of playing golf in Vermont.

After the game, we had a tasty lunch at the clubhouse restaurant. The food and service were great. After our meal, I went outside again just to take a look at the scenic view and to snap some pictures.

A couple of weeks later, I received an email from the Gokarna Forest Resort where they asked me if I had enjoyed the round of golf and my time there. This was a thoughtful customer service approach, and of course, I replied to their email, saying I had enjoyed my golf round and was very happy with the service as well.

What a Trip: This is Nepal, where I grew up, kids (Wash Post)

Who: Binod Thapa (the author) and his son and daughter, AJ and Monica, all of South Riding, Va.

Where, when, why: We traveled to Nepal the first two weeks of January. I am originally from Nepal and have always wanted to take my children there.

Highlights and high points: The kids had the most fun going on an elephant safari in Chitwan National Park at dawn. It was cold and foggy, but we saw mom and baby rhinos, various kinds of deer, and boars. The kids loved it.

Another highlight was our Himalayan Mountain flight. Initially, it was delayed for more than an hour because of fog. Finally, after long and anxious anticipation, the fog cleared, and the plane took off. We were able to see Mount Everest up close as well as a number of the tallest mountains in the world. It was amazing and exciting but also gave me a sort of peaceful feeling.

Cultural connection or disconnect: I am from a big family. My grandparents have twelve children and many grandchildren. This was the first time that my children had met many of their cousins and other relatives, but it didn't take long for them to connect with them. They felt as if they'd known them all along.

Biggest laugh or cry: Initially, we were all excited to go canoeing in Chitwan National Park. We enjoyed canoeing on the Rapti River and being able to see lots of crocodiles sunbathing. But it was a little scary because the boat was long but fairly narrow and a little unsteady, and we worried about tipping over—with all those crocodiles right there!

Another time, we were visiting an elephant breeding center in Chitwan National Park when all of a sudden one huge wild elephant came out of the jungle. The tour guide told us that this elephant had killed a man two weeks earlier and warned us to stay far back. He told us that we were lucky to see it, since the wild elephants didn't usually come out this far. But whenever the animal moved, we ran in the opposite direction.

How unexpected: I am from Nepal, but I had not visited some of these places and experienced some of these activities before. I love nature and could spend days trekking in the Himalayas. We had a plan to visit a number of places in

Nepal, and we covered most of it. We went to Biratnagar in the southeast, in the plains closer to India. We also went to Pokhara, west of Kathmandu. In the mountain village of Sarangkot, at dawn, we saw the most breathtaking sunrise and mountain views.

Fondest memento or memory: Being able to bring my children to the country where I was born was very gratifying and was made more joyful because they loved Nepal and had a great time.

*This article first appeared in the Washington Post.

EUROPE

MALAGA, SPAIN, EUROPE – 3/23/2016

Golf Course Name:	Parador de Málaga Golf
Address and Website:	Autovía MA-20 (Málaga-Algeciras) Salida-1, 29004-Málaga, España T + 34 951 011 120 F + 34 952 372 072 malaga.golf@parador.es www.parador.es
Country's Players/ People:	Garcia, Margarita
Comment:	*Nice playing with you and good luck in your world golf adventure!*
Highlight:	My favorite parts of this trip were playing golf by the seaside and traveling with my daughters. What a memorable trip!

Monica was in a study abroad program in Malaga, Spain, for six months. In March of 2016, Serena and I visited her. While I was there, I played one round of golf at the Parador de Malaga del Golf.

The staff members were friendly, and I played with a gentleman who was very polite. This golf course was by the Mediterranean Sea on the right, and there were some holes right by the seaside. We enjoyed a countryside view as well as a beautiful view of the Mediterranean Sea. This golf course was decent, but their greens were absolutely beautiful! As a matter of fact, their greens were probably the best I have seen so far—impeccably maintained! The course was mostly flat, so not that challenging and easier to play. Both of us played fairly well. We also took a few pictures together, and he offered to take a few pictures of me on the golf course.

After the round, we exchanged our phone numbers and email addresses. Usually, I like to buy the club's logo items after the round, but there weren't many items to buy, so whatever they had, I bought one of each. Before I left the golf course, I went back by the Mediterranean Sea and took a few more pictures. Because this course was by water and the greens were absolutely stunning, this was one of my favorite courses I played across the seven continents.

While we were in Malaga, my daughters and I took a ferry from near Gibraltar to Tangier, crossing the Mediterranean Sea. I believe the distance was only forty kilometers from Spain, Europe, to Morocco, Africa. There was probably a total of twenty-five to thirty people on the tour. We got an all-inclusive deal from Marriott, so when we were in Morocco, we didn't have to bargain or pay money. The tour was quite well-organized.

Once we arrived in Tangier, a tour bus picked us up and took us to different parts of the city, stopping in some historic places. In one place, we rode on camels. Monica and Serena enjoyed the camel ride.

The tour guides also took us on a two-kilometer walking tour in the middle of the city. The funny thing was the street vendors! As soon as we started walking, probably eight to ten vendors started following us, trying to sell their products. The tour guide had warned us about this and instructed us on what to do ahead of time, which was very helpful. Vendors followed us for the two-kilometer walk. They were not aggressive, but it was funny that they followed us the entire time.

Personally, I like to buy local merchandise from the vendors instead of buying at the store. The price is better, but most importantly, you are supporting the local economy and the poor. I usually also like to buy things exactly at the place where I visited. For some reason, it feels like I am getting authentic items. That's what I do wherever I travel.

While we were in Tangier, we had an interesting walk around the area. The tour bus and guide took us to some historic parts of the city, including to where we took our camel ride, and we had an enjoyable authentic lunch. The city near the harbor and the water looked just beautiful. It was hard to believe we were in Africa.

We left Tangier around six in the evening and arrived near Gibraltar around seven. It took about an hour to cross from Africa to Europe on the ferry. From the middle of the Mediterranean Sea, we could see a beautiful view of Africa on one side, and on the other side, we could see Europe. The water looked gorgeous! We arrived in Malaga around nine in the evening. It was a very productive and eventful day!

We also spent a few days each in Madrid and Barcelona. I thoroughly enjoyed the traveling with Monica and Serena!

Fifty Capitals Golf Courses

No.	Capital and State	Golf Course	Date
1	Bismarck, ND	Hawktree Golf Course	5/25/2017
2	Pierre, SD	Hillsview Golf Course	5/26/2017
3	Cheyenne, WY	Prairie View Golf Course	5/28/2017
4	Lincoln, NE	Highlands Golf Course	5/29/2017
5	Harrisburg, PA	Dauphin Highlands Golf Course	6/24/2017
6	Juneau, AK	Mendenhall Golf Course	6/29/2017
7	Olympia, WA	Capitol City Golf Club	7/1/2017
8	Salem, OR	Salem Golf Club	7/2/2017
9	Boise, ID	Boise Ranch Golf Course	7/3/2017
10	Helena, MT	Fox Ridge Golf Course	7/4/2017

Played Golf With	Contact Info
Fred S. (Member)	(701) 355-0995 3400 Burnt Creek Loop Bismarck, ND 58503 http://hawktree.com/
Bill R. (Member)	(605) 773-6191 4201 SD-34 Pierre, SD 57501 https://www.cityofpierre.org/124/Golf
Ken B.	(307) 637-6420 3601 Windmill Rd Cheyenne, WY 82001 http://airportgolfclub.com/
Jim M. and Son (Members)	402-441-6081 5501 NW 12th St. Lincoln, NE 68521 http://lincolncitygolf.org/
Cord H., Bill B., Douglas S.	(717) 986-1984 650 S Harrisburg St Harrisburg, PA 17113 https://www.golfdauphinhighlands.com/
Brian S. and Brad K.	(907) 789-1221 2101 Industrial Blvd Juneau, AK 99801
Richard, Tony, Justin	(360) 491-5111 5225 Yelm Hwy SE Olympia, WA 98513 http://www.golfcapitolcity.com/
Randy and Linda	(914) 669-5485 2025 Golf Course Rd, S Salem, OR 97302 https://salemgolfclub.com/
Roger C. and Rob H.	(208) 362-6501 6501 S Cloverdale Rd Boise, ID 83709 http://www.boiseranchgc.com/
Dave F.	406-227-8304 4020 Lake Helena Drive Helena, Montana 59602 https://foxridgegolfcourse.com/

No.	Capital and State	Golf Course	Date
11	Richmond, VA	Glenwood Golf Club	7/22/2017
12	St. Paul, MN	Highland National Golf Course	9/1/2017
13	Madison, WI	Bridges Golf Course	9/2/2017
14	Des Moines, IA	Waveland Golf Course	9/3/2017
15	Springfield, IL	Lincoln Greens Golf Course	9/4/2017
16	Annapolis, MD	US Naval Academy Golf Club	9/24/2017
17	Trenton, NJ	Trenton Country Club	10/28/2017
18	Raleigh, NC	River Ridge Golf Club	2/24/2018
19	Dover, DE	Maple Dale Country Club	4/1/2018

Played Golf With	Contact Info
Pete T. Jimmy B.	(804) 226-1793 3100 Creighton Rd Richmond, VA 23223 http://www.glenwoodgolfclub1927.com/
Front Nine: Dan and Lynn E. (Son and Father) Back Nine: Greg, Joey	(651) 695-3774 1403 Montreal Avenue St Paul, MN 55116 https://stpaul.golf/ https://stpaul.golf/highland-national-gc/
Ann N. and Jacque Mark H. (Member)	(608) 244-1822 2702 Shopko Drive Madison, WI 53704 http://www.golfthebridges.com/
Scott and Brian S. (Father and Son) Dan D.	(515) 248-6302 4908 University Ave Des Moines, IA 50311 https://golfwaveland.com/
Bill and Dave Kimsey (Father and Son)	(217) 786-4111 700 E Lake Shore Dr, Springfield, IL 62712 http://springfieldparkdistrictgolf.org/lincoln_greens_golf_course/
Lonnell Fears	410-293-9747 44 Greenbury Point Rd Annapolis, MD 21402 https://usnagolf.com/
Chung L. Virgil M., Buddy	Brian, (609) 883-3800 201 Sullivan Way Trenton, NJ 08628 www.trentoncc.com
Andrew R. and Steve	(919) 661-8374 3224 Auburn Knightdale Rd, Raleigh, NC 27610 www.golfriverridge.com
David and Chris R. (Father and Son)	302-674-2877 180 Maple Dale Circle Dover, DE 19904 http://mapledalecc.com/

No.	Capital and State	Golf Course	Date
20	Nashville, TN	Harpeth Hills Golf Course	4/20/2018
21	Frankfort, KY	Frankfort Country Club	4/21/2018
22	Charleston, WV	Berry Hills Country Club	4/22/2018
23	Sacramento, CA	Cordova Golf Course	5/24/2018
24	Carson City, NV	Silver Oak Golf Course	5/24-25/2018
25	Salt Lake City, UT	Bonneville Golf Course	5/26/2018
26	Denver, CO	Overland Park Golf Course	5/27/2018
27	Santa Fe, NM	Santa Fe Country Club	5/28/2018

Played Golf With	Contact Info
Andrew T. and Andy S.	615-862-8493 Kevin Pro Shop 2424 Old Hickory Blvd Nashville, TN 37221 https://www.nashville.gov/Parks-and-Recreation/Golf-Courses/Harpeth-Hills-Golf-Course.aspx
Kevin J. and Al N.	502-695-1400 101 Duntreath St Frankfort, KY 40601 www.frankfortcountryclub.com
Ganpat T, Jashvant, Danny S.	304-744-1393 1 Berry Hills Rd Charleston, WV 25309 www.berryhillscc.com
Steve A., Lee, Ben, Frand and Phil (Father and Son)	Pro Shop – 916-362-1196 9425 Jackson Road Sacramento, CA 95826 www.cordovagc.com
Bryan, Mike and Ryan (Father and Son) Wendy Ryan and Jim	Pro Shop – 775-841-7000 1251 Country Club Drive Carson City, NV 89703 www.silveroakgolf.com
Joe C., Adam and Danny	Pro Shop – 801-583-9513 954 Connor Street Salt Lake City, UT 84108 https://www.slc-golf.com
Craig and Charles	Pro Shop – 720-865-0430 1801 S. Huron Street Denver, CO 80223 https://www.cityofdenvergolf.com/overland-park/
Rudy and Cliff	Pro Shop – 505-471-0601 4360 Country Club Road Santa Fe, NM 87507 www.santafecountryclub.com

No.	Capital and State	Golf Course	Date
28	Phoenix, AZ	The Legacy Golf Club	5/29/2018
29	Lansing, MI	Groesbeck Golf Course	6/16/2018
30	Indianapolis, IN	Eagle Creek Golf Club	6/17/2018
31	Columbus, OH	Champions Golf Course	6/18/2018
32	Austin, TX	Riverside Golf Course	7/3/2018
33	Baton Rouge, LA	Santa Maria Golf Course	7/4/2018
34	Jackson, MS	Live Oaks Golf Club	7/5/2018
35	Little Rock, AR	War Memorial Golf Course	7/6/2018
36	Oklahoma City, OK	Lincoln Park Golf Course	7/7/2018

Played Golf With	Contact Info
Dave S., Tony and Fred	Pro Shop 602-305-5550 6808 S 32nd Street Phoenix, AZ 85042 www.golflegacyresort.com
Rodney and Darrell Robert and Bill (Father and Son)	Pro Shop – 517-483-4333 1600 Ormond Lansing, MI 48906 www.groesbeckgolfcourse.com
Tom S. and Brian M.	Pro Shop – 317-297-3366 8802 West 56th Street Indianapolis, IN 46234 www.eaglecreekgolfclub.com
James C. and Justin M. Greg	Pro Shop – 614-645-7111 3900 Westerville Road Columbus, OH 43224 https://crpdgolf.com/golf-courses/champions-golf-course/
Jeremy S. Mike W. and Roy H.	Pro Shop – 512-223-6677 1020 Grove Blvd Austin, TX 78744 www.riverside-gc.com
Matt S.	Pro Shop – 225-752-9667 18460 Santa Maria Pkwy Baton Rouge, LA 70805 http://golf.brec.org/courses/santamaria/
Jim C.	Pro Shop – 60-982-1231 11200 US 49 Jackson, MS 39209 www.liveoaksgc.com
Dustin, Josh and James	Pro Shop 501-663-0854 Little Rock, AR 72205 www.warmemorialgolf.com
Richard and Ricky (Father and Son)	Pro Shop 405-424-1421 4001 NE Grand Blvd Oklahoma City, OK 73111 www.okcgolf.com

No.	Capital and State	Golf Course	Date
	Holts Summit, MO	Railwood Golf Club	7/8/2018
37	Jefferson City, MO	Oak Hills Golf Center	7/9/2018
38	Topeka, KS	Lake Shawnee Golf Course	7/9/2018
39	Augusta, ME	Western View Golf Club	8/31/2018
40	Montpelier, VT	Montpelier Elks Country Club	8/31/2018
41	Concord, NH	Concord Country Club	9/1/2018
42	Boston, MA	George Wright Golf Course	9/1/2018
43	Providence, RI	Triggs Memorial Golf Course	9/2/2018
	Hartford, CT	Buena Vista Golf Course	9/2/2018

Played Golf With	Contact Info
Chris C. and Joey H.	Pro Shop 573-896-4653 12925 County Rd 4037 Holts Summit, MO 65043 www.railwoodgolf.com
Tom P. and Doug	Pro Shop 573-634-6532 932 Ellis Blvd Jefferson City, MO 65101 https://www.jcparks.com/facility/oak-hills-golf-center/
John B. and Derrell D.	Pro Shop 785-862-0114 4141 SE East Edge Rd Topeka, KS 66609 https://lakeshawneegolf.com/
Aaron S., Jim H., Ken T.	(207) 622-5309, Pro Shop Pete, 130 Bolton Hill Rd Augusta, ME 04330 https://westernviewgolfandpub.com/
John R. and Sampson A.	203 Country Club Rd, Montpelier, VT 05602 (802) 223-7457 https://vtga.org/portfolio-item/montpelier
Mike D. and Les S.	22 Country Club Lane Concord, NH 03301 (603) 228-8936 www.concordclub.org
Preston M. and Nick N.	420 West Street Hyde Park, MA 02136 617-364-2300 www.cityofbostongolf.com
Bob and Dave N.	1533 Chalkstone Ave, Providence, RI 02909 (401) 521-8460 https://triggs.us/index.php
Woody and Bob	37 Buena Vista Rd West Hartford, CT 06107 (860) 521-7359 https://www.westhartfordct.gov/town-departments/leisure-services/buena-vista-golf-course

No.	Capital and State	Golf Course	Date
44	Albany, NY	Wolferts Roost Country Club	9/3/2018
45	Tallahassee, FL	Hilaman Golf Course	9/29/2018
46	Montgomery, AL	Aroostook Golf Course	9/29/2018
47	Atlanta, GA	Browns Mill Golf Course	9/30/2018
48	Columbia, SC	Oak Hills Golf Club	10/1/2018
49	Honolulu, HI	Honolulu Country Club	10/28/2018
50	Hartford, CT	Goodwin Park Golf Course	5/11/2019 5/12/2019

Played Golf With	Contact Info
J. David M. and Robert K.	120 Van Rensselaer Blvd, Albany, NY 12204 (518) 449-3223 www.wolfertsroost.com
Nick M. and Christian T.	2737 Blair Stone Rd Tallahassee, FL 32301 850-891-2560 www.hilaman.com
Shawn L.	1501 Dozier Rd Montgomery, AL 36117 (334) 260-4900
Harry J. and Terrance D.	480 Cleveland Ave SE Atlanta, GA 30354 (404) 366-3573 www.cityofatlantagolf.com
Jim K., Manny C., and Don M.	7629 Fairfield Rd Columbia, SC 29203 (803) 735-9830 www.oakhillsgolf.com
Ross and Debbi W. Lynn T.	1690 Ala Puumalu St, Honolulu, HI 96818 https://www.honolulucountryclub.com/index.php
Alex and Liz	1130 Maple Avenue Hartford, CT 06114 860-543-8518 www.goodwinparkgolfcourse.com

Seven Continents Golf Courses

No.	Continents	Golf Course	Date
1	North America	South Riding Golf Club	8/19/2000
2	Africa	Mirage City Golf Club	10/16/2011
3	Australia	North Ryde Golf Club	11/4/2012
4	South America	Juan Bautista Segura Municipal Golf Course	3/9/2013
5	Antarctica	Prospect Point	3/15/2013
6	Asia	Gokarna Forest Resort Golf	10/8/2014
7	Europe	Parador de Málaga Golf	3/23/2016

Contacts Info	Comments
43237 Golf View Dr, South Riding, VA 20152 (703) 327-6660 http://www.southridinggc.com/	My club. Great staff and great members. A great golf course!
Ring Road, New Cairo, Egypt Tel – 2409-1464 https://www.marriott.com/hotels/hotel-information/golf-courses/cai-jw-jw-marriott-hotel-cairo/	A beautiful golf course!
137-207 Twin Rd, North Ryde NSW 2113, Australia https://www.northrydegolfclub.com.au/cms/ office@northrydegolfclub.com.au Tel - 61 2 9887 4422	It was great to see my cous-in-brother Kanchan after almost ten years!!
C1429 Buenos Aires, Argentina Tel – 4772-7261 and 4774-9158 https://buenosaires.gob.ar/desarrol-loeconomico/deportes/golf-en-el-campo-de-la-ciudad	Playing golf and meeting great people was special!
G Adventures https://www.gadventures.com/	It was a great feeling to hit and swing at golf balls in Antarctica.
http://www.gokarna.com/golf Ward No. 5, Kathmandu, Bagmati 977-1-4451212	Very pretty golf course. I enjoyed playing with my cous-in-brother and his friends at this course.
Autovía MA-20(Málaga-Algeciras) Salida-1, 29004-Málaga, España T + 34 951 011 120 F + 34 952 372 072 malaga.golf@parador.es https://paradores.es/en/parador-de-malaga-golf	These are the best golf greens I have played! The fact that it was alongside the Mediterranean Sea made this course beautiful!

SUMMARY

Simply put, it has been a tremendous journey. Meeting people from different parts of the country and the world, exploring beautiful and historic sights and locales, and combining my love of golf, travel, and learning has been the most gratifying experience.

My journey has been more than just a series of golf trips. For me, these travels were also very helpful in terms of understanding people and the culture of different regions. During these travels, I met so many wonderful and unforgettable individuals, many of whom I am keeping in touch with. I have invited them here to the D.C./Virginia area, and some of them have already come. When they visit, they meet my family, but I also bring them to our golf club to play one round of golf with our members and friends. Bonding and forming meaningful relationships with people from all around the globe are what matter the most!

Traveling and seeing beautiful parts of the country and world has been an absolutely amazing experience as well. In the U.S., some of my most memorable highlights include breathtaking views of Mendenhall Glacier in Alaska; beautiful green mountains and crystal-clear lakes in New England; miles and miles of beautiful farms in Idaho; the gorgeous mountains of Montana; Standing Rock Indian Reservation and crossing the Dakota Access Pipeline; and the gorgeous water views in Hawaii. It was all just beautiful!

From an international perspective, seeing the Himalayas in Nepal, playing golf by the Mediterranean Sea in Spain, walking around the Giza Pyramid in Egypt, visiting Buenos Aires in Argentina, seeing kangaroos and koala bears in Sydney, and crossing the Antarctic Circle have been my highlights.

All in all, this has truly been the journey of a lifetime, and I'm so glad I have the opportunity to share it with those who supported me along the way and with you, reader. Now, you've been a part of my journey too!

I would like to thank all of those friends who encouraged and supported me throughout my travels, particularly the SRGC staff and members, the Friday Night League players, and all my friends. I would also like to thank all the players with whom I golfed in all fifty U.S. states and on all seven continents.

Obviously, I would have liked it if Nora could have accompanied me on my travels. We have never left the kids with grandparents or other family members even to go on a short vacation, let alone embark on long domestic and overseas trips. So I totally understand why she couldn't come along. Plus, Nora is not a golfer, and sometimes, my golf travels are hectic. Either way, I'd like to thank Nora for her unwavering support for my passion and journey. I would definitely not have been able to accomplish it without Nora's help and encouragement. I always appreciate my children, Monica, AJ, and Serena, for their interest and encouragement as well! Thanks also to all my uncles, aunts, sisters, and brothers.

I couldn't have done any of this without help from so many family members and friends! You are all part of this journey, and I am forever grateful!

Acknowledgments

FAMILIES

In 2021, Nora started a fun project. On Christmas, each family member needed to present a story that was connected to the family. In essence, we needed to showcase how significant the story was in the family and describe how we are thankful for each other. During Christmas of 2022, I presented my first golf story. There's no doubt my travels and experiences were connected to my family—and I am forever grateful to them.

With that in mind, I would like to begin by expressing my deepest gratitude toward my own family. I'd like to thank Nora for genuinely supporting my golf journey to all fifty U.S. state capitals and seven continents. Without my wife's help, I wouldn't have been able to complete my journey. Her support was monumental, and it was a big part of my success—and I am thankful for that. Second of all, I'd like to say thank you to Monica, AJ, and Serena. Their encouragement and support played a significant role in my journey as well.

I'd also like to thank my extended family members—uncles, aunts, brothers, sisters, cousins—who were always encouraging.

MY CLUB

I just wanted to say thank you to our GM, Jon, for all his help and support throughout my journey. Jon has been a big help, and I genuinely thank him for all his support! I'd also like to thank our head golf pro, Andrew. He is a very polite and creative person, and I appreciate all his help. I would also like to thank Chad who helped me during my golf journey. Thanks to Pete, Katie, Sonia, Garham, Mollee, Morgan, Sonia, Hanseong, Joe, Sean, and Jay. I would also like to thank Jim M., John H., Dave A., Brad, Carroll, Jack S., Ben C., Charlie, Jim O., Terry, Jeff C., Gordan, Mason and Joy, Kevin P., Larry M., Bill, Mike R., Harley, Ben H., Vince, Zack, Nicole, Les W., Stan, and all other friends for their encouragement of my travels. Finally, I'd like to say thank you to all other members and friends at my club for their encouragement and friendship!

FRIDAY NIGHT LEAGUE (FNL)

Thank you very much for all your encouragement during my travels to seven continents and fifty capitals!

I have been running the Friday Night League (FNL) at my club for the last eight years. It's the best league! I have a great group of players—they are entertaining and make the league better. It's been great knowing all the guys and gals. They are all appreciative of what I do for the league, and I appreciate them.

I'd like to thank all FNL players, including Nick, Bob, Lonnell, Larry B., Ken, Andy, Justin, Geoff, Matthew, Uttam, Kenny, Corey, Pat, Scott M., Charles, Dae, Ed, Kevin M., Dean, Eric, Jeff B., Ruben, Christina, Courtney, Brian, Jerry, Chris, Trevor, Brandon, Mike, Larry G., Mason, Dennis, Jeff H., Deron, George, Scott R., Jack, Katie, Howard, Dallas, Kevin P., Mason C., Joy B., Robert M., Gary D., Dustin, Terry, and Scott L., for their encouragement and support.

Others

I would also like to thank Gary W., Pat M., Turner, Al C., Phil, Chuck, Don, Ed, Alex, Greg, Andy, Kevin, Justin M., Mario, Todd, Greg, Heath, Russ, Kevin M., Earnie H., Al, Erric K., David R., John D., Hugh, Joanie, Dean P., Shannon, Brett, Duane, Leonard, Jeff T., Herb, Barbara, Lisa R., Don, Alex, Fred, Mario, Hugh, Joannie, and John as well as Raju Bhinaju, Bishwa, Bijay, Bimal, Sunil, Bobby, Sunita, Devendra, Hari, Udaya, Pratap, and Anup.

Last but not least, special thanks go to Damber and Punya (uncles), Sharada Didi, Narayan (brother), Sridhar Dai, and Nick G.! They were the most encouraging, communicative, and supportive of my journey.

Organizations

Titleist – I played with Titleist clubs and golf balls in all fifty U.S capitals and on seven continents. I have always used them.

VSGA – Virginia is my home state, and VSGA is a golf organization. During my U.S. golf travels, I brought along their magazine and took pictures in front of and around their clubhouse. With it being my home state and the golf organization of the state, I felt it was important.

South Riding Proprietary – We live in the community. Bringing an "SR" sticker and taking a picture in front of all fifty U.S. capitols was good way to remember my community.

Marriott – I stayed at Marriott hotels and their properties in the U.S. and worldwide.

Since I played with Titleist equipment in the U.S. and across the world, I carried VSGA magazine and SR sticker across the U.S., and I stayed at Marriott worldwide during my golf adventure, these organizations were all part of my golf journey. I am thankful for that!